Those Three Years

COVID-19, One Doctor's Journey, and

A Prescription for National Healing

By: Paul Bunge, MD

Those Three Years: COVID-19, One Doctor's Journey, and a Prescription for National Healing. Copyright © 2025 by Paul Bunge. Self-published in Ferndale, Washington.

Printed in the United States of America

First edition, December 2025

Book cover design by Jennifer Bunge

Editing by Eddy Hall. Proofreading by Megan Waldner

Library of Congress Control Number: 2025914611

ISBN: 979-8-9993702-0-4 (hardcover)

www.thosethreeyears.com

Contents

An Invitation

Unless you slept through the COVID pandemic, you noticed that people often disagreed about how best to respond to it. During those three long years, I listened to hundreds of people's stories. I share some of those stories in this book. I didn't agree with all that was said, but I learned something from each of them.

In this book, I share my story from my perspective, my background, my experience. Your story is different, and if you would care to share it with me, I would love to hear it. You probably won't agree with my perspective on every issue. If that happens, I invite you to make a mental note and keep reading. If I learned anything during COVID, it is this: listening to those we disagree with has value. If we don't communicate, not only do we stagnate spiritually and emotionally, but we are more likely to get hurt or die.

I tell the stories of many people who did amazing things, and I wish I could have told more. But what I want the most is for us to heal. To do that, we need each other. My hope and prayer is that reading this book will be a spiritual journey for you, as writing it has been for me. You may not view things the same way I do once you finish this journey, but perhaps we will find each other along the way and become friends.

Chapter One: The ICU

We know that we have passed from death to life…
– I John 3:14 (NIV)

You matter because you are, you matter to the last moment of your life…
– Cicely Saunders[1]

A s I watched, the green glowing heart monitor lost its rhythm, replaced by random waves and spikes as if it were attached to a Labrador puppy. But it was my father on the other end of those wires, unconscious and bloated grotesquely by fluids his body could no longer get rid of. It didn't look like he had much time. Suddenly, the puppy went quiet. Flatline is not a tough diagnosis, even if you're barely 15 years old and you have never seen a heart monitor. My mother was wandering about, not sure what to think or feel. I wasn't much better: my first time in an ICU, my dead father lying there, my uncle in the hallway. My father's ventilator continued to raucously pump air into his lungs. It seemed insulting to his already beat-up body to make it seem alive, like Frankenstein. My mother might be emotionally paralyzed right now, but I talked to the nurse. It took some time for her to find a

---

[1] Cicely Saunders (1918–2005) was an English nurse, social worker, physician, and writer. She is well known as the founder of the modern hospice movement. See: Wikipedia contributors, "Cicely Saunders," *Wikipedia*, *The Free Encyclopedia*; 2024 Nov 2, https://en.wikipedia.org/w/index.php?title=Cicely_Saunders&oldid=1254960386.

resident doctor who could approve turning off the vent. Peace and quiet at last. So much more appropriate, more honoring to his leaving, and respectful of the hole in our hearts he left. It was 1983. I was still in high school, and it would be 12 years before I would graduate medical school. That day in the hospital pointed my life in a direction. I have since spent myself saving lives, helping the suffering, comforting families, squeezing years from science, and trying to give people like my father more time with their loved ones.

I am an Internist. That means I have been trained in internal medicine, with three years of residency after medical school. Internists in the US most often work as primary care doctors for adults, or as hospitalists: caring for those sick enough to require time in a hospital. About half of those who train in internal medicine sub-specialize in areas such as cardiology, nephrology, critical care, and infectious diseases. Although I also have certification in palliative care, I consider myself a general internist.

Before COVID arrived, I was working at both Providence St. Peter Hospital in Olympia Washington, and Providence Centralia Hospital, about 30 minutes to the south. My workday in Centralia starts with overnight handoff. Dr. Lam really wants to go home at 7 AM and hopes the daytime doctors will come in a little before that so he can tell them about the patients he admitted. I have had plenty of night duty in the past and I appreciate the feeling. I arrive at 6:50 AM after a half-hour drive through the rain that I have made every wet winter to one hospital or another for the last 18 years. Dr. Lam tells me the brief version of two patients' stories and I ask a few clarifying questions. One "chest-pain-rule-out," meaning someone with chest pain but so far, no obvious heart attack identified by EKG or labs. The ER docs are worried enough that they want him watched. He may need a treadmill or nuclear study. Is he on a heparin drip to thin the blood and prevent heart attacks? No, not worrisome enough to risk giving that medication right now.

The other patient is a woman with dementia from a nursing home. She has aspiration pneumonia again. I just saw her a couple of months ago: no family to make decisions for her, no longer talking. The court-appointed guardian is loath to take a more palliative approach, not wanting to shirk her duties to the patient, which I understand. At the same time, she suffers so, coming to the hospital again and again.

I spend the next hour looking up labs and vital signs for the patients on my team. All the records these days are in "Epic," the electronic medical record (EMR)[1] for the hospital, and it does everything but flush the toilet. This means nurses, doctors, and other staff must interact with it for hours each day: entering results, putting in notes, ordering tests, sending requests for consultation, everything. This is the first hour of what will probably be about five total of my interacting with a screen today, along with my other duties.

Once I have reviewed the information, printed my list, and have a basic understanding of the patients on my team, I venture out to see them. At any time, I might be called by the nurses or the ER about an urgent issue or a new admission. An admitting doctor will come in for a "swing shift" at 11 AM, but before that (and after as well, if too many patients come in at one time), we can be called to the ER. The rest of the day is a massive game of multi-task. See your patients, examine them, talk to them, come up with a plan, and send them home if appropriate. In the meantime, field calls from nurses, families who want to ask something, specialists who you want to talk to or who need to talk to you, administrators who need to have meetings about quality and time and staff happiness, and your spouse who reminds you to text her once or twice to remind her that you love her even though you are busy. And otherwise, handle any emergencies that come up.

First stop, ICU. The Intensive Care Unit in Centralia is a five-bed unit that has become less and less ICU-level over the years. The complicated cases are sent to larger hospitals. As doctors become more specialized in knowledge and work focus, small town hospitals suffer. Papers are published showing that patients with strokes and trauma and other problems do better in specialized centers in big cities, so they are shipped there. This means the smaller hospitals become less and less familiar with these cases, and the published papers become self-fulfilling prophesies. Yet not everyone can or wants to be shipped out of town for their care.

---

[1] Epic is a private software company, with headquarters in Wisconsin. www.epic.com.

I put those thoughts aside and see my patient in the ICU: Mr. Charlemagne, here for cirrhosis with bleeding varices. The liver, when diseased to the point of cirrhosis, in this case from alcohol and hepatitis C, becomes a clogged filter for the blood passing through it. The liver is supposed to process blood coming from the gut, pulling out toxins and acting as a catalytic converter for the vast array of chemicals that are in food, water, and even medications. Without a liver, the body is quickly overwhelmed and poisoned. A cirrhotic liver still functions, but weakly, and with so much scarring, the blood physically backs up. The pressure goes to the two ends of the gastrointestinal system and veins in the esophagus and the rectum start to swell. These "varices" in the esophagus can rupture. When that happens, the patient may bleed to death quickly. I know my patient has not yet had an endoscopy to look for varices, because Centralia's only GI doctor is out of town. Other doctors on duty are only able to do diagnostic endoscopy; they can look to see what the problem is, but lack the training to do the interventions needed (in this case, possibly banding the varices--putting a kind of rubber band on them to stop them from bleeding).

Mr. Charlemagne would have been sent to a larger hospital, but there is a problem: no beds available at St. Peter's. It is time to continue the multi-task game. At least I can skip looking up phone numbers on Google because Donita is on duty as ward clerk in the ICU today, and she will check again with hospitals in Vancouver or Longview. I have worked with Donita for nearly 20 years, and I know she won't forget. Beds, though, are not the only issue. That hospital's GI doctor will need to approve, and often they hesitate to take on these challenging patients. Bleeding is difficult to control, the patients are at high risk of dying anyway, they sometimes lack housing, nursing homes won't take them, and alcohol withdrawal symptoms can be difficult to manage. But I will need to convince a GI doc if I want to give Mr. C a chance.

I visit Mr. Charlemagne, and he is mostly coherent today. The Ativan is keeping the withdrawal symptoms at a manageable level. The blood transfusion he had last night has put his hemoglobin up to 7.5 so he doesn't need another unit just yet. He is willing to go out of town if we can find a bed for him. While Donita starts calling hospitals, I head out of the ICU to 2 South.

Providence Centralia Hospital is mostly one elongated box with two floors. There are two units on each floor (1N, 1S, 2N, 2S), plus the ICU off the middle of the second floor. The first floor also has OB, ER, cafeteria, lab, etc. My life is mostly the four units, the ICU, and the ER. 2S is step-down, meaning some higher-level care but not quite ICU. 2N and 1S have general nursing capabilities. 2N is more medical-focused, and 1S is more surgery-focused, with most of the post-op patients. 1N has more long-term patients and has changed over the years from official nursing home status to caring for the patients waiting for a nursing home bed as the backlog has increased.

On my list today are three potential discharges, likely to go home or to a nursing home. I need to see them next. If I don't start on the discharges, the social workers won't have time to coordinate transportation, the families will be annoyed, and the hospital will have more meetings about length of stay and time of discharge.

Mrs. Lovelace is not awake at 8:30 am. A gentle tap on the shoulder must be repeated before she opens her eyes. "Hello young man," she says sweetly. She is doing much better, and very importantly she is no longer on oxygen. She has not been up and about yet, but a quick stop at the nurse's station produces a pulse oximeter and off we go. After making sure her oxygen doesn't drop with walking and she is able to get around with the walker, it is time to get back on Epic. After years of using it, this grandiose name of the EMR still amuses me. It's an "Epic discharge" when people go home. A scheduled reboot requires "Epic downtime." When Epic changes something at their headquarters in Wisconsin, they call it an "Epic upgrade." I do an "Epic reconciliation" of Mrs. Lovelace's heart failure medications and send the new Lasix dose off to Walgreens pharmacy electronically. Her daughter will be at the hospital at 10 to pick her mom up. My work on the discharge summary is interrupted by morning medications. The nurse needs to use the computer to record the meds, so I sign off and find another one at the nurse's station to finish up. Before the EMR, I pushed around a stack of charts from room to room, which was more efficient for me, though I would sometimes get calls when the clerk could not decipher my calligraphy. The current system has eliminated that problem at least.

My pager goes off. It is the ER with a cellulitis case. That should be easy enough. On my way down, I stop at the doctor's lounge for a bagel with peanut butter. While there, I am paged by a pharmacy—yesterday's prescription for a blood pressure medication won't be covered by the patient's insurance, is it OK to change to another one? Sure. I am in the hallway when Donita's page comes through: you better get on the phone with this specialist now, or you will lose your chance. I race the rest of the way to the ER: anyone who has worked at rural hospitals knows well one of the biggest challenges is transferring patients out. You have about as much standing as if you were crossing an international border: the doctor must be honest, straightforward, appreciative, succinct, and clear, or it is not going to happen. They may ask you questions, berate you, question your intellect, challenge your integrity, and you can only say yes and thank you. In the end, you are left belittled, and know people talk about you: that small-town doctor, what does he know? Confidence is not my strong point. As I swing into the ER, I see Dr. Kevin Caserta talking to a group of nurses. Kevin is the medical director for St. Peter Hospital in Olympia as well as Providence Centralia Hospital. I wonder: *is it worth it to pay doctors to try to manage nurse's complaints?* How can I have condescending pride and a self-confidence problem wired together into my skull?

I borrow a phone at the ER desk—my cell reception is horrible in Centralia.

"This is Doctor Fourier, GI." I explain Mr. Charlemagne's situation. "Don't you have GI there?" Dr. Fourier asks irritably.

I remember I am advocating for my patient, not myself. "We only have partial coverage. Today we only have the general internist who can't do banding. Also, we don't have platelet access currently and he is very low on those."

Dr. Fourier hems and haws but in the end, his yes starts the transfer machinery going between the two hospitals. They have room and will take my patient today. I see the cellulitis patient and scurry back to the ICU to transfer Mr. C out.

My day continues. I talk to and examine the rest of my list of patients. Write orders and notes. Talk to families. Discharge some people, one to a nursing home. A couple of discharges are delayed: a nursing home bed is not ready, and one patient is not quite strong enough yet. I sneak some lunch in from the doctor's lounge soup choices. In the afternoon multidisciplinary meeting, I review my list with the case managers and the head nurses. If I finish up my notes before 6 PM, sometimes I can go for a short run. Not today. I head home at 7:30 PM. My wife Jennifer has stories from her day, and she has saved me some dinner. After that, a little reading, then search for sleep. The kids are now all out of the house: David an accountant in Bellingham, Erika a medical scribe in Seattle applying to med schools. Nathan a freshman at Washington State University in Pullman, loves the marching band and his friends. I don't need to stay up and read them books anymore. I miss that, but appreciate the sleep.

Next day, same schedule. Five new patients on the team from admissions yesterday and overnight. Another new patient waiting for me in the ER. So the day progresses, the weeks, the years. It is not easy to see everyone in their pain and suffering. But what an honor and a privilege to be able to comfort, to clarify the problem, and bring a solution. Antibiotics for infection, fluids and supportive meds to bring people back from the edge, blood thinners and stents for heart attacks. People tell their doctors what they tell nobody else. Sometimes, you would rather not hear it, but most of the time, it is a great honor when people tell you their secrets in the hope that this or that will help bring them health.

In many ways, it is like any other job: do the work, fill out the paperwork, check all the boxes. Make sure that the team knows your plans, and you know theirs. Take the time to educate the patient and their families and find out what their decisions and plans are. At the end of the day, make sure your list is all up to date for the night team and, if you are going off service, the next doctor coming on. Answer questions about coding and billing.

Overall, this is work that I love. I am paid essentially for my opinion: how great is that?

I love other work as well. I also enjoy seeing patients in the clinic. I have enjoyed the many times I have volunteered overseas. I have also been in medical leadership, with some successes, and some maybe not so much.

The field of medicine for me has never been only a job or a set of transactions. It has always been a calling, an assignment, a ministry. Just as my father served God as a Lutheran pastor to the farmers and others in rural America and Canada, I have seen my work and my role as the way God has led me to serve. This is one of the greatest honors available to us, in whatever our field of work, to be what St. Paul describes as "God's handiwork." Paul says that God created us to do good works, which he "prepared in advance for us to do."[1] As such, we broken and imperfect people become part of the masterpiece that God, the perfect artist, is fashioning.

In January of 2020, news was stirring about a new virus from China, but we were not sure yet what to make of it. I followed the story closely, reminded of the West Africa Ebola outbreak, and how I had volunteered to go help with safety training in Liberia. At the same time, I followed my mother's progressive memory loss. She was still living by herself in Canada, with visiting caregivers I had arranged.

---

[1] Ephesians 2:10 (NIV)

Chapter Two: Arrival

So the Lord sent a plague on Israel...
— I Chronicles 21:14 (NIV)

Everybody knows that pestilences have a way of recurring in the world;
yet somehow we find it hard to believe in ones that crash down on our
heads from a blue sky. There have been as many plagues as wars in
history; yet always plagues and wars take people equally by surprise.
— Albert Camus[1]

There was plenty to do at the hospital in Centralia in early 2020. The hospital was full as a busy flu season was underway. My patient lists were long and the days flew by. By early February, a heavy dread lay over the whole hospital: our state confirmed the first case of the new coronavirus in the United States on January 20, 2020.[2]

A young man had recently arrived from the area around Wuhan, China. He was hospitalized at the Providence Hospital in Everett, just north of Seattle. Governor Inslee reassured us in public announcements that there was no need for alarm: the current isolation procedures were

---

[1] Albert Camus, *The Plague*, trans. Stuart Gilbert (Vintage Books: 1972), 35.
[2] "COVID-19 Timeline," David J. Sencer CDC Museum: In Association with the Smithsonian Institution, accessed March 19, 2025, https://www.cdc.gov/museum/timeline/covid19.html, I used this web page for other timeline-related events as well in this book.

more than adequate. His speech and the related talking heads were a distraction as I rounded on my patients. Even if you turned off the volume for the patient you were seeing, the blare continued from the roommate's TV. I wanted to listen, but the patient with cancer in front of me took priority.

It seemed unlikely that this new virus would amount to much. The thinking was that person-to-person transmission was rare, and most of the cases were from people who had been exposed to animals at the Wuhan seafood market.[1] Quarantine, case investigations, and contact tracing would be key to keeping this new virus at bay. The CDC stumbled with testing early on, which put us behind, but I was confident these world medical experts in Atlanta would pull it together. Working with local public health officials, they would have no problem with the basic interventions needed. In fighting the virus, several factors were on our side, including what we thought was a low risk of an infected person giving it to someone else. So long as each person with the virus infected fewer than one other person on average, we would be fine. This is how a virus surge dies out, no matter how bad the outbreak.[2] The other thing in our favor was that the new virus surely would not infect others until the person carrying the virus was symptomatic. We would only need to screen for symptomatic people from China at this point.[3]

While this was going on, my mother's memory was worsening. After she lost her driver's license, I hired caregivers for a few hours most weekdays. She complained about it but was doing OK for many months. But now, the caregivers were calling me: she was using the stove and

---

[1] "CDC confirms first US case of Wuhan coronavirus in Washington State," *MyNorthwest News*, January 21, 2020, https://mynorthwest.com/1678441/wuhan-coronavirus-washington-state-cdc/.
[2] If $R_0=1$, then the number of patients would typically stay steady, as each infected person on average infects 1 other person. $R_0>1$ means on average more than 1 person is infected, which means the number of patients will grow and grow and grow. For example, if $R_0=2$, then 1 patient infects 2 people, then they infect 4, and those infect 8, and pretty soon you have a very large number of sick people indeed.
[3] It was not until September 14, 2020, that the CDC ended symptom-based COVID screenings of air travelers, citing limited effectiveness due to asymptomatic spread. "COVID-19 Timeline."

leaving it on. Her ability to keep the house was getting worse and worse, and she wouldn't allow the caregivers to do more than they were already doing. She was more confused, and it was time for a new plan.

I went to my mother's home in Edmonton, Alberta, and flew with her to my sister's house in British Columbia. We had placed her name on the waiting lists of a couple of assisted living facilities there, but she would stay with my sister for now. Who knew the difficulties that these facilities would face during the COVID pandemic? Who knew the border would be essentially closed to us for months and I could not help with Mom's care? For now, we left her belongings in Edmonton and asked her friends to keep an eye on things. The next week, I was back at work in Centralia.

In mid-February, the World Health Organization (WHO) named the new virus "COVID-19," which I will refer to as "COVID." At the end of February, Evergreen Hospital near Seattle diagnosed a seriously ill man with COVID. He died on the first of March. A nearby nursing home had several cases, which was big-time news. Obviously, these elderly people had not visited Chinese seafood markets. It was transmitting person-to-person, and it was in our state. Doctors and nurses were even more on edge.

I talked to a doctor-friend at the Evergreen hospital, 80 miles north of Centralia, to prepare myself emotionally for COVID patients and get some tips. We had so many patients with viral illnesses at Centralia Hospital at the time, but COVID testing was still difficult to get. As far as we knew, we did not have any COVID-19 cases. But when one of the ambulance drivers from that same nursing home was sick on our wards, I guessed we were having cases but not diagnosing them. We were directed to not wear masks, as Seattle and other places where there were known cases were higher priority. Finally, after several nurses complained, we were allowed to bring in homemade masks. Friends starting sewing. A good friend made caps with buttons on the sides so you could wear the mask all day without hurting your ears—just loop over the buttons. These caps were an amazing gift, especially later, when mask-wearing was a 15-hour-a-day experience.

I rapidly became frustrated with the approach that our medical system and society in general were taking. I asked someone in hospital leadership about this:

"I know people in the community are slow to accept masking," I said. "I know wearing a mask outside of surgery feels odd for Americans. But shouldn't we do more at least in the hospital? We are both preventing disease and being an example to others."

"Don't worry, Paul," he said. "You are far away from COVID down here, there won't be any cases."

What went through my head at that point was: You have to have people in leadership who are reassuring and comforting. That's an advantage. But this should be balanced with a realistic concern that we may very well be starting on a serious new medical problem. But I kept that part bottled up. He was already laughing at my thought that our testing may not be accurate, so I didn't bring up stricter protocols for gowning and gloving, preparing for COVID cases, and the like. From my experience with Ebola and what we knew from the history of SARS, I knew this was not the way to eliminate a virus at the early stages and prevent a global pandemic. But this approach, and my internal frustration, would continue nationwide as platitudes substituted for action.

I was haunted by another picture from the 2014 Ebola crisis. Many of the clinics around Liberia's capital city of Monrovia also served as low-level hospitals, with a few beds for patients with illnesses as well as maternity cases. We would visit these clinics and train staff in how to use protective gear, wash with diluted chlorine, safely dispose of sharps, and reduce infection risk while delivering babies (Ebola causes early delivery and miscarriage).

One day, we were looking for a particular clinic and were told that it was closed. But if we wanted, we could talk to that man under the palm tree. The man, Howard,[1] was the husband of the clinic director. Howard told us that his wife had delivered a stillborn baby from a sick mother about a month ago. Then she and other staff became ill. They were now in the Ebola treatment center run by Doctors Without Borders. It was not clear if she would live. He himself had been directed

---

[1] I use pseudonyms throughout the book as appropriate.

to quarantine for 21 days and report if he developed any symptoms. More than two weeks later, though he was feeling fine, here he was under the palm tree keeping his distance from us. I wondered at the time whether Americans would be so disciplined or self-sacrificing if we faced a similar catastrophe in our country. The people of Liberia, Sierra Leonne, and Guinea worked diligently to contain that horrible disease, and the outbreak was eventually conquered. Because of their hard work, the rest of the world was not at significant risk of catching Ebola in 2014 and beyond. Now it was our chance to return the favor. Would we rise to the challenge?

The WHO published an extensive report at the end of February 2020, outlining how to contain COVID-19, based on China's experience.[1] This report contained inaccuracies due to the Chinese government's lack of transparency about origins and their initial response, and because much was not yet known about how the virus was transmitted and how it would behave. But the report was crystal clear on two things: first, steps all governments and healthcare systems could take now to interrupt the spread; second, a warning that if the world did not implement these strict and challenging interventions, the virus could assault the entire planet, with a death rate between 0.5% and 6% of those infected.

Working at St. Peter's one day, I asked a friend why the United States did not take this and other advice from the World Health Organization seriously. I had known this doctor since he was a young teen. He had grown up in both Asia and the US. I also knew he had thought a lot about East-West relations and opinion patterns. "Hubris," he said.

"Hubris?" I repeated, confused.

"Hubris. We are much too proud to take advice from the WHO and the Chinese medical community." You could tell he was implying there was a racist vein in this attitude, along with a national and cultural

[1] Bruce Aylward et al., *Report of the WHO-China Joint Mission on Coronavirus Disease 2019 (COVID-19)* (World Health Organization, 2020), https://www.who.int/docs/default-source/coronaviruse/who-china-joint-mission-on-covid-19-final-report.pdf.

superiority complex. "People think: what does China know anyway? It's their fault this virus is here! It should be named the Wuhan virus! That is why we as a country did not jump on this report and quickly implement lockdowns and re-focus the medical system toward testing, contact tracing, and isolation." The consequences of our slow response would play out in patient after patient, death after death, statistic after statistic, as the months went on.

Krista and Patrick Hastings are good friends of ours in Tacoma, Washington. In early March of 2020, Krista's grandfather caught COVID, one of the early cases in Snohomish County, Washington.[1] Patrick kept me updated on the grandfather's case. He was in the ICU for 10 days but survived. Krista had visited him at home just before the diagnosis, and they called me for advice. I walked them through a quarantine approach for the family, and they took it seriously. They stayed only in the house and yard for two weeks and nobody got sick. They were so excited to get together with others again. But the day their quarantine ended, with known cases in the state at 1,000, Governor Inslee issued the state-wide stay-at-home order.

I had a new job: interpreter of news reports to family and friends. Walking Patrick and Krista through their exposure was the first of many such discussions over the phone, Zoom, and in person. I was reading all I could about the virus in medical journals and online. The infectious disease doctors at St. Peter's, especially Dr. Standaert, became a lifeline to the rest of us. The information was coming so rapidly, it was difficult to sift through. These specialists had more direct connections to the CDC and the IDSA (the Infectious Diseases Society of America), and they were often able to get updates before the rest of us could. For several months, Dr. Standaert gave regular updates to the hospitalists on the status of the disease and current treatments.

I posted some updates on Facebook and a blog. I gave Zoom lectures to community groups and college classes. This was before large amounts of misinformation had come out, and people were generally interested

---

[1] "Death toll rises to 11 in Washington as cases reach 70," *KOMONEWS,* March 5, 2020, https://komonews.com/news/coronavirus/snohomish-county-residents-should-avoid-gatherings-of-50-or-more.

and receptive. It is easy to talk when people accept what you are saying—one's opinion flows without effort with the knowledge that the responses will all be "yes." But if we only speak to those who agree with us, and we only listen to our own reflected opinions, that type of communication is incomplete at best. How much of our inability to listen to each other now is due to what we lost during COVID, and how can that be healed?

In March, both hospitals where I worked had their first confirmed cases of COVID.[1] The first documented positive COVID-19 case in Thurston County—where St. Peter's is located—was March 11. Lewis County, home of Providence Centralia Hospital, confirmed its first case March 15. Now my morning list had COVID patients on it. Not much change for the doctor's actual day: see and examine patients, only now with a disposable gown forming a cloud of yellow fluff around you so you look like a big Easter treat, capped with a white PAPR. The PAPR (Powered Air-Purifying Respirator) has a small fan to push air through an N95 filter on your waist, attached to a tube running to your head where the air blows down from the top of a bicycle-helmet-shaped cap with a see-through face tent attached. It does not need to be specially fitted to your face like an N95 mask does, and it can be reused. After the Ebola scare, hospitals generally favored maintaining PAPRs over N95 masks in case of emergency. I had never thought that was a good idea since you can only have so many PAPRs, and they are complex to maintain. But rules on N95 masks require everyone in the hospital to get a fitting every year, so it was easier for hospitals to maintain a few PAPR devices instead—so long as you didn't actually need them. Those hospitals that chose PAPRs probably thought they would never be deployed in large numbers, beyond their occasional use for a patient with suspected TB on the wards. How wrong they were.

The PAPR is more comfortable than an N95 mask. Because the tight-fitting N95 mask takes some force to breathe through, it can physically wear you out. But the PAPR has its own problems: you can't wear it all day because the battery only lasts so long, and you can't hear

[1] See Chapter 3 regarding COVID testing in early 2020 and the University of Washington's work. This suggests we probably had local cases sooner than March but could not diagnose them accurately.

well due to the rush of air blowing by your ears. When you use a stethoscope, especially the cheap disposable ones you are supposed to use in the COVID rooms, you are pretty much guessing what things sound like since it is not quiet enough for a good exam.

The infection control crew at Providence worked hard to train us in donning (putting on your protective gear) and doffing (taking off your protective gear). But it took a while for everyone to get into the swing of such extensive protection. I was reminded again of the Ebola caregivers in West Africa. There, donning and doffing were performed outside, with a separate person to rinse you off with sprays of chlorine. That would have worked for COVID also—a simpler and less expensive way. But the American healthcare system is not about cheap: it is about liability (who will pay for the damaged lungs from chlorine?) and comfort (we want breathable gowns that are waterproof). In any case, the kinks were worked out, and we continued as yellow Easter chicks, me at 6 foot 4 inches plus the noisy white cap on top.

The hospital and our group tried to limit COVID exposure among staff and between patients by assigning only one or two doctors to all the COVID patients and trying to keep them mostly in one area of the hospital. Not everyone was excited about taking their turn on the COVID teams. Some were caring for elderly parents at home. Some were simply nervous, understandably. I've always accepted that there is some risk involved in practicing medicine. I thought long and hard before I accepted a Navy scholarship for medical school—being in the military has risks, even though in the medical department the risks are low. But once I decided, I decided, risks and all. You sign up for the good and the bad. You can't pick and choose after the fact.

Practicing medicine for me has always been about saving lives when possible, from the day my father's puppy-heart stopped. That does not mean I have no fear of dying. I was so nervous when COVID came to Washington State. But I did not find it hard to take a COVID team at the hospital, to volunteer as a tester in Seattle, or to go to Liberia during Ebola, for that matter. Doing something about a problem seems to calm me down and help me focus, instead of letting worried thoughts swirl about my head. Working is a way to face your fears. Having already lived a decade longer than my father did, what bothers me more than my death, which is inevitable, is the thought that I may have left something undone, something unsaid, some question unasked, that put someone at risk.

With that passion, I became a regular annoyance to the hospitals' administration during COVID. What could we do better? How could we encourage masking? What about cleaning the floors in the COVID rooms? When would we get masks? How about N95s? I could only bother them so much. My other outlet became the punching bag I had set up in the garage for my youngest son who enjoys boxing. It was not getting any use since Nathan had gone off to college, but in those first six months of COVID, the punching bag and I both got quite the workout. I alternated between imagining it was a hospital administrator, a conspiracy theorist, a church leader who defied masks, and the president. It was a great way to burn some calories and lessen how much trouble I got into at work and in the community. A channel for my anger issue, but not a solution to it.

Again, during this first COVID phase, I remembered the early months of Ebola. The hard work of so many to educate and convince people, many of whom had never seen a microscope, to believe that something invisible was a danger to them and their families. And that what they did, as individuals and more importantly as communities, could make a real and important difference in their lives and the lives of the whole world. I remember dining with a group of men after everyone's long day; highly educated scientists working with the WHO in Liberia, talking about community education with local tribal chiefs. What it meant to have such an impact through listening and understanding. And what impact it had on them—well-off urban black men from cities in the US and elsewhere—to connect with these rural chiefs from another time and place, but who were in a way their fathers and brothers. Could we do the same? Could our communities be just that—communities? People who see each other as valuable enough to give time to each other, seek wisdom from each other, and make a way forward together to fight this virus? Or would our tiny enemy find the weakest links in our chain and become a truly worldwide pandemic?

Chapter Three: The Lab

Sow your seed in the morning, and at evening let your hands not be idle, for you do not know which will succeed, whether this or that, or whether both will do equally well.

– Ecclesiastes 11:6 (NIV)

Gandhi lived his life as someone convinced that his decisions about how to live mattered and that he had the power to make those decisions conform to what he believed right.

– Sissela Bok[1]

I t's like one of those terrible moments you occasionally see if you watch the Olympics on TV. A great runner, with an excellent chance of winning a medal, is about to start. The contestants are lined up, waiting in complete silence for the starting signal. Feet are properly placed in the starting blocks. Bulging muscles, honed over years of careful training, glisten in the sun, ready for action. Our runner is ready, trained, motivated, well coached, and especially patriotic. But as soon as the gun blasts and the runners leap up and start, our champion stumbles. His ankle twists wildly, his mass of muscles becoming a useless weight that only tears his tendons as he goes down in a heap.

---

[1] Sissela Bok, forward to *Gandhi, An Autobiography: The Story of My Experiments with Truth*, by Mohandas Ghandi, trans. Mahadev Desai (Beacon Press, 1993), xvii.

Early on in COVID, like our tragic runner, the US stumbled disastrously when it came to COVID testing. If the glorious American medical system, with its well-trained doctors and nurses, with its array of tests and treatments, was to rise to this new and dreadful challenge, it had to develop COVID testing as its first step. But the system fell apart when it should have sprung into action. Delayed diagnosis cost many lives. This embarrassing stumble brought a great loss of credibility from which public health in America never recovered through the rest of the pandemic. However, unlike our runner, some amazing people quickly picked up the pieces and got running anyway, despite the late start.

Dr. Zhang Youngzhen, a laboratory professor from China, worked with Dr. Edward Holmes from the University of Sydney to make the original COVID genome public on a virology website on January 10, 2020.[1] Labs across the world raced to use this information to make their own tests for the virus and started using their tests on cases such as ill patients coming from China. But the FDA, trying to ensure accuracy, announced a new rule on February 4, 2020, requiring all American labs to request and obtain specific emergency approval before using any test for COVID they themselves developed. At the same time, the CDC used the information from Zhang and Holmes to make a COVID test, and their test was the only one initially given authorization for use by the FDA.[2] Test kits were sent out to multiple public health labs but were quickly found to be inaccurate in multiple settings. The CDC's test needed much more work before it would be clinically useful. The

---

[1] Charlie Campbell, "Exclusive: The Chinese Scientist Who Sequenced the First COVID-19 Genome Speaks Out About the Controversies Surrounding His Work," *Time*, August 24, 2020, https://time.com/5882918/zhang-yongzhen-interview-china-coronavirus-genome/

Note that Dr. Zhang was later punished for his work by the Chinese government: Smriti Mallapaty, "Chinese virologist who was first to share COVID-19 genome sleeps on the street after lab shuts," *Nature*, May 1, 2024, https://doi.org/10.1038/d41586-024-01293-0.

[2] Robert Baird, "What Went Wrong with Coronavirus Testing in the U.S.?," *The New Yorker*, March 16, 2020, https://www.newyorker.com/news/news-desk/what-went-wrong-with-coronavirus-testing-in-the-us.

CDC's botched test and the FDA's impulsive decision effectively blocked accurate COVID testing in the United States for precious weeks. Our country's medical system failed right at the beginning of the pandemic.

One of our country's heroes who picked up the pieces was Dr. Alex Greninger, professor of pathology at the University of Washington in Seattle. Always interested in science, he became one of those nerdy, ultra-intelligent few with both an MD and a PhD by the time he graduated medical school from the University of California in San Francisco. He knew from the start that he wanted to work in the lab, unlike so many medical students who discover their love for the microscope after a good bruising from the personalities, quirks, drama, culture, and dialogue of the live human specimen. When COVID came along, after spending many years doing research in virology, with an interest in RNA viruses, and work with SARS, he felt like a football player with many years of experience who finally found himself at the Super Bowl. You train for it your whole life, dream about it, try to get ready, not knowing if you will ever get there. What else could you do but face it head-on, work your hardest, and try to win?

Seeing the necessity of quick and accurate testing for COVID, Dr. Greninger and his team started working on a test using the genome as soon as it became available online. Every day of delay would translate into more deaths, how many they could not know. They worked steadily through one weekend to validate the test. The seemingly endless process was complete by Sunday morning. After that, Alex swung by the assisted living facility to pick up his mother and her clothing. His mother-in-law was already staying in the apartment with him and his wife because she could not get back overseas where she lived. But he felt a duty to reduce his mom's risk of catching COVID and relieve her of the difficulty of lockdowns and isolations that so many institutionalized elderly faced during that time. The moms took turns on the couch through that summer.

Their test worked well, and Dr. Greninger's team began the onerous submission process to the FDA, which they had to guess at because of the change in policy.[1] They were able to use their tests on patients, but not until the beginning of March, after many phone calls, emails and faxes to the government (the FDA later streamlined the process after receiving so many complaints). In contrast, the public health laboratory in Alberta, Canada, was using their accurate homegrown test by the end of January 2020,[2] more than a month sooner.

In the hospital, we felt like something was off, but we moved on, assuming we had access to the best information we could get. We were like most clinicians, oblivious to the struggles Dr. Greninger and the rest were facing. But I felt a great discomfort, feeding the boiling anger and frustration inside me, which I can see now was my desire to save lives. My inner alarm, planted the day my father died, was as loud as a foghorn in my ears, but it seemed like no one else could hear it. Was I crazy? Was I overreacting? I certainly was confused.

Though they were initially delayed by government bureaucracy and had to become part-time lobbyists, once they finally received approval for their test, Dr. Greninger's lab expanded its capabilities and accepted samples from all over the state. I remember trying to figure out, even months later, how to get COVID samples to the national commercial laboratories for testing (Labcorp and Quest). By then, these national labs had some capability for testing, but their lab collection sites would not see patients for testing. In addition, they refused to take the samples I brought them—even double bagged and chlorine washed.

In the meantime, Dr. Greninger and colleagues made the University of Washington lab a powerhouse of COVID testing. Soon outgrowing their usual space, they expanded the lab to take over several floors in other buildings. Unlike the federal bureaucracy, the university and his colleagues were very supportive of their work.

I asked Dr. Greninger about these issues much later:

---

[1] Julia Loffe, "The Infuriating Story of How the Government Stalled Coronavirus Testing," *GQ*, March 16, 2020, https://www.gq.com/story/inside-americas-coronavirus-testing-crisis.

[2] Kanti Pabbaraju et al., "A Public Health Laboratory Response to the Pandemic," *Journal of Clinical Microbiology* 58, no. 8 (2020), https://doi.org/10.1128/JCM.01110-20.

"Alex, you really struggled with the FDA and the CDC, these large federal bureaucracies. What do you think of our country's system of regulating medical care? Generally speaking, do you think it would be better done at the state or federal level?"

"There are many disadvantages when the states all make different rules," he replied wisely. "In this case, however, the CDC and the FDA became single points of failure, which impacted the entire country—even the whole world—during the pandemic. When you're dealing with an exponentially growing problem like a pandemic, you have to change the playbook as no one person or group can keep up on their own."

Alex Greninger put love into action. Working in the lab, he did not have to put on an N95 mask and navigate the COVID rooms of the hospital. He could have focused on writing scientific papers from his home office and distracting himself with Netflix. Instead, this man cared enough, believed enough, was brave enough, to battle every day for what he knew was right. For what would save lives. Though he saw no patients in person, his work resulted in over 5.7 million tests run.[1] No clinical doctor could see that many patients in those three years and give answers to their questions like Alex did.

As more COVID patients came in, in brutal waves but also with slow time between waves where the hospitals were relatively empty, the pressure increased on the care teams, as well as the hospital leadership. Administration had to schedule more staff when it was busy and cut back on staff when it was light. It was so disruptive to everyone. According to one survey, 18% of healthcare workers quit their jobs between February 2020 and September 2021.[2] Travel nursing as a field grew even more than before, as hospitals had more of a challenge to fill staffing slots when needed.[3]

---

[1] Alex Greninger, personal correspondence.

[2] Abby Vesoulis and Abigail Abrams, "Contract Nurses are Making Big Money in the Age of COVID-19. Are They 'Exploiting' the Pandemic?," *Time*, February 23, 2022, https://time.com/6149467/congress-travel-nurse-pay/.

[3] Jean Lee, "Travel nurses' gold rush is over. Now, some are joining other nurses in leaving the profession altogether," *NBC News Online*, September 3, 2022, https://www.nbcnews.com/health/health-news/travel-nurses-gold-rush-now-are-joining-nurses-leaving-profession-alto-rcna45363.

Our medical director, Dr. Kevin Caserta, visited the wards frequently, listening to the nurses vent their frustrations. Small-town nurses can be like the best of country songs: in one continuous stream, they review failed relationships, family trials, community gossip, hospital politics, and the latest antics of their golden retriever, putting it all out on the table. COVID added the stressors of masks, risks, and crazy schedules to the mix. What could Kevin do but stand there, patiently listen, and reassure? How could he possibly translate the masterpiece of poetry just unloaded onto him into some meaningful sentence he could take back to the boardroom?

In the midst of this, the patients who had a hard time socially faced even more challenges. A Spanish-speaking patient with COVID was feeling better but still required oxygen. He couldn't stand the hospital food, and his son would drop off meals intermittently at the front of the hospital. A simple thing, but it seemed to take congressional coordination to get that food to him, with visitors restricted and staff confused as to how to manage interactions between patients and the outside world. I was walking in from the parking lot one day and recognized the son. After plenty of pointing this way and that between us without a common language, he seemed convinced that I would take the food upstairs, which I did.

I took care of my patients, but when I considered how many Americans were getting sick and dying, I was angry. Why couldn't the American public be at least as conscientious and work together as the Africans did during Ebola? After decades of telling the rest of the world how to do public health, why couldn't our world-class institutions rein in this virus? I was taking it out on the punching bag, trying to learn from the leadership classes I was taking. I could identify my anger as one of my significant weaknesses, along with my problem with low self-confidence ironically partnered with pride. These issues had made me less effective over the years in conveying my ideas and in leading, and I was trying desperately to keep them in check. Could I put into action what I had been learning at the seminary: lean on God instead of my own moral sensitivities, work effectively with others even without completely agreeing with them, and love the knuckleheads as much as Jesus does?

Chapter Four:
The Hospital and the Treatments

...and he sent them out to proclaim the kingdom of God and to heal the sick.

– Luke 9:2 (NIV)

They [healers of various stripes] satisfied that eternal human need for hope of relief, for sympathy, for taking action, which is felt in times of suffering.

– Leo Tolstoy[1]

C aring for COVID patients is both extremely simple and very complex. For many, it only causes a severe cold, like a multitude of other viruses. But a significant minority gets very ill. When it hits those with underlying diseases, it can cause them to worsen. The worst COVID cases occur when a massive inflammation in the lungs makes the patient unable to breathe on their own. This is typically in the second stage of COVID, after the body has begun to recover from the virus, but then gets worse. Much of the problem in this stage is an overreaction of the immune system to the virus. At this stage, the COVID patient may require hospitalization and oxygen, or even high-flow oxygen or a ventilator. Most recover, but many worsen, usually gradually. Those

---

[1] Leo Tolstoy, *War and Peace*, trans. Ann Dunnigan (Signet, 1968), 790.

who eventually die often spend another one to three weeks in the ICU first as the doctors and nurses try their best, knowing they can save some. It is a long slog for the patient, for the family, for the medical folks, only to end in death for many.

Caring for patients with COVID as a non-ICU hospitalist was not all that technically complicated if COVID was all they had: give them oxygen and watch for complications. If they were too ill at the Centralia hospital, we intubated them and mostly sent them to the ICU in Olympia, or if that hospital was full, down south to Longview. Some went to OHSU[1] in Portland or UW[2] in Seattle where they could get "ECMO." Extracorporeal Membrane Oxygenation is a way of pushing the patient's blood through a membrane where it is infused with oxygen. It is a complicated system that temporarily replaces the function of the lungs. It was effective for some COVID patients, especially the younger ones who would have died without that extra oxygen.

For every COVID patient who needed a ventilator or ECMO, many would not require that level of support, though they were sick enough to be in the hospital on oxygen. With oxygen and other support, most pulled through. In many countries with less access to oxygen, many of those people died.

In Centralia and St. Peter's, we took our turns on the COVID teams. These patients were in the hospital much longer than the average patient—COVID is a disease that is not in a hurry. We would see them day after day, though they were isolated from other patients and their families. In America, we have spent so much on private rooms and semi-private rooms, though psychologically and practically it would have made much more sense to room these folks in an old-fashioned open ward where they could interact with each other instead of spending 2 weeks alone or with 24-hour news stations as their only companions. We watched them and cared for them, and if they got worse, we sent them off to the ICU. When they improved, we sent them home, sometimes on home oxygen for a while. High-flow

---

[1] Oregon Health Sciences University Hospital.
[2] University of Washington Hospital.

oxygen is a relatively new therapy that helped many COVID patients avoid the ventilator. It requires a machine that heavily humidifies and warms the oxygen so that when you give it at a whopping 60 liters per minute into someone's nose, it doesn't damage their airway by drying it up. I watched a heavyset Samoan American man in his thirties sitting in his chair on one of these systems, talking cheerfully and perfectly coherent. Without it, he would have been dead within minutes.

At first, we had no proven COVID-specific medications. The first therapies that most people thought would be useful were hydroxychloroquine and remdesivir. They both have been around for a long time, one as a medication for parasites and autoimmune disease, the other a complicated-to-make antivirus medication that never found itself a role in medicine. Both showed some promise in the lab against COVID. Hydroxychloroquine was relatively cheap and available as a pill, and doctors started using it, especially after the FDA's emergency approval based on limited studies in March of 2020.[1] Research labs around the country stopped what they were doing and started studying hydroxychloroquine. A flood of results soon showed hydroxychloroquine was worthless for COVID, and most providers quit using it. This is not unusual: many therapies show promise in the lab but show no benefit after enough testing in actual patients. Because so many studied it at once, hydroxychloroquine may hold the world record as the drug most scientifically disproven for a particular purpose. In spite of conclusive findings, some people still insist on using it for COVID patients.

Remdesivir was expensive and used in the hospital with some benefit to the patients and a big payoff to the manufacturer, Gilead, though most of its development was funded by the government.[2] The FDA initially blessed it only for "compassionate use," an odd category where a medication can be approved for one individual patient at a time,

---

[1] Paul Offit, *Tell Me When It's Over: An Insider's Guide to Deciphering COVID Myths and Navigating Our Post-Pandemic World* (National Geographic Press, 2024), 44.
[2] Catherine Thorbecke, "Coronavirus drug remdesivir to cost $3,120 per patient with private insurance, irking critics," *ABC News*, June 29, 2020, https://abcnews.go.com/US/covid-19-drug-remdesivir-cost-3120-us-patients/story?id=71509977.

in this case only in the hospital. It also was used because of its potential benefit, but without clear evidence at the time. I thought enrolling patients in a study would have been more beneficial than the "compassionate use" category. When the government opens a door for the use of a medication before it is proven, there is financial pressure to push that door open wider and wider. Remdesivir is now approved for inpatients with COVID, but this later summary of the evidence helps to clarify the problem:

> Data from randomized trials do not clearly or consistently demonstrate a major clinical benefit with Remdesivir among hospitalized patients overall, although there may be a benefit for a select subgroup of patients with severe disease who are not on ventilatory support at the time of treatment initiation.[1]

"Compassionate use" is a kind of victory for the individual ("I want something now; I am not going to risk getting a placebo!") over benefit to the community. Remdesivir was later shown to benefit high-risk outpatients in preventing hospitalization,[2] but requires three days of IV therapy, which made it difficult to give in the outpatient setting.

Steroids were used on many patients to try to reduce the inflammation of COVID. They were later shown to be helpful in sick hospitalized patients in rolling back the overactive immune system, which is the main pathological problem by the time the typical COVID patient is sick enough to be in the hospital. But giving steroids to them too soon, such as to someone not requiring oxygen, was found to possibly make the COVID patient worse.[3]

---

[1] Arthur Kim and Rajesh Gandhi, "COVID-19: Management in Hospitalized Adults," *UpToDate*, ed. Connor R. F. (Wolters Kluwer), accessed October 3, 2024.
[2] R. L. Gottlieb et al., "Early Remdesivir to Prevent Progression to Severe Covid-19 in Outpatients," *New England Journal of Medicine* 386, no. 4 (2022), 305, https://doi.org/10.1056/NEJMoa2116846.
[3] Preliminary results of the RECOVERY trial were out by June of 2020: The RECOVERY Collaborative Group, "Dexamethasone in Hospitalized Patients with Covid-19," *New England Journal of Medicine* 384, no. 8 (2020), 693–704, https://doi.org/10.1056/NEJMoa2021436.

Proning is a therapy with minimal to no side effects.[1] Proning is simply laying on your stomach instead of on your back when you are in bed. Laying on your back makes it harder for your lungs to expand freely, but when lay on your stomach, the lungs are suspended from the back and they can work with less restriction. This allows the lungs to oxygenate blood more easily and heal more quickly. Proning has been used for years in the ICU, typically when someone is ventilated due to ARDS (acute respiratory distress syndrome). It is difficult to prone someone who is on a ventilator, but specialized beds and equipment have been designed to make it possible. For the non-intubated patient, it helps to have a lot of pillows under the legs and elsewhere to help people adapt. Though it is a simple therapy, because the nurses were not used to it, and later there were questionable study results, the hospitals were slow to implement it.

We used convalescent plasma at the beginning of COVID, but not very much. This refers to the immune components in the plasma of people who have recently recovered from COVID (or other infections). This type of therapy pre-dates antibiotics, and for COVID, it was first used in Wuhan, China.[2] There was some initial evidence that it helped, but more time and more studies grouped together did not show clear benefit in hospitalized patients.[3] Later, drug companies developed targeted antibodies copied from some of the ones in convalescent plasma, and these will come up again. Studies soon started on other anti-COVID therapies, drugs that did not exist for other reasons pre-COVID, but these new medications would take some time to develop and test.

---

[1] Hanyujie Kang et al., "Effect of Awake Prone Positioning in non-Intubated COVID-19 Patients with Acute Hypoxemic Respiratory Failure: A Systematic Review and Meta-Analysis," *Journal of Intensive Care Medicine* 37, no. 11 (2022), 1493–1503, https://doi.org/10.1177/08850666221121593.

[2] Chenguang Shen et al., "Treatment of 5 Critically Ill Patients With COVID-19 With Convalescent Plasma," *Journal of the American Medical Association (JAMA)* 323, no. 16 (2020), 1582–1589.

[3] Claire Iannizzi et al., "Convalescent Plasma for People with COVID-19: A Living Systematic Review," *Cochrane Database Systematic Reviews* 5, no. 5 (2023), https://doi.org/10.1002/14651858.CD013600.pub5.

As time went on, I found myself spending more time with the COVID patients. Most patients in the ICU were sedated. But the ones I was caring for on the medicine wards were bored, lonely, scared, and frustrated that they couldn't be home with their families. As I had time, I tried to visit them beyond the time I needed to be there, so they would have someone to talk to. Of course, it was annoying for both of us that I was in a PAPR (or later, N95 mask), and it was hard to talk to each other. I also couldn't stay long. But so many people seemed to appreciate the time I spent. I was reminded of a very simple book of my father's (I have many of his old theology books), written for hospital chaplains, *The Ministry of Listening.*[1] The message is simple: listen to people. You don't need to preach to them for God to use you to give them hope. This applies to doctors as well as chaplains. Whether you are encouraging someone to lie on their stomach in the hospital, stop smoking, take their medications, go to church, or be kind to their spouse, the first step is always listening.

Most of my time and energy in March and April of 2020 went into the slog of patient care as the COVID patients kept on coming. Whether I was on a COVID team or a regular one, we all lived with the constant worry that we might catch COVID and possibly get very sick and die. It was like a weight bending you over, or a constant tightness around your chest. We became obsessive: wiping down our cell phones and pagers, avoiding others, masks on top of masks, avoiding the COVID teams or floors. Every day I saw people, especially the nurses who spent the most time with them, caring for the COVID patients with fantastic courage. They confronted their fears the way Martin Luther King Jr. urged: face them honestly and question why we fear, manifest courage that acknowledges fear and pulls it inside oneself to process, and then master that fear through concrete steps of love and faith.[2]

To make room for the many COVID patients, hospitals stopped doing elective surgeries. My hospitals did not have to treat people in tents like they did in New York, though many times space was tight. My

---

[1] Donald Peel, *The Ministry of Listening* (The Anglican Book Center, 1980).
[2] Martin Luther King Jr., *Strength to Love* (Fortress Press, 2010), 119–131. I strongly encourage reading this book, especially this chapter about fear.

role during this time was "per diem" status for the hospitals in Centralia and Olympia. That meant that I was not guaranteed regular work, and only worked when I agreed. With the heavy patient load, I was working more than full time. I often talked with the public health doctors in Lewis and Thurston counties about how to advise patients when they went home to their families, how to connect people for contact tracing, and how to reduce the risks to nursing homes. I knew there was more public health work we should be doing to manage this outbreak. Was there more that I could do?

Chapter Five: A New York Minute

The eyes of the Lord are on the righteous, and his ears are attentive to their cry.
— Psalm 34:15 (NIV)

Courageous acts are not performed by people with a personality trait called courage. Courageous acts are performed by normal people who passionately believe in what they are trying to do.
— Tim Irwin[1]

P ortia Redfeather has been an ICU nurse for decades. I met her in Haiti, where we both volunteered with Project Medishare.[2] It was just months after the massive 2010 earthquake, and the medical needs still ran very high. I felt privileged to work with someone so professional, positive, compassionate, supportive, and endlessly kind. We stayed "friends" on Facebook with her frequent posting of her family and her hobbies from her home in North Florida, long after Haiti.

As COVID was ravaging New York City in the spring of 2020,

---

[1] Tim Irwin, *Run With The Bulls Without Getting Trampled*, (Nelson Business, 2006), 61.
[2] Project Medishare, a non-governmental organization started by Drs. Barth Green and Arthur Fournier in 1994, still works in Haiti. Www.projectmedishare.org. See also: Enrique Ginzburg, et. al., "Rapid Medical Relief—Project Medishare and the Haitian Earthquake," *New England Journal of Medicine* 362, no. 10 (March 11, 2010), e31, https://doi.org/10. 1056/NEJMp1002026. Note Portia and I volunteered several months after this initial response.

Portia noticed advertisements asking for nurses to go and help. Together with a nurse friend, she signed up for a two-week stint. She recalls an intense draw to respond to the glaring need. Naturally, everyone feared for her, including her petrified husband, but she carried amply supplied emotional support along with her scrubs and stethoscope.

Portia and her friend received night assignments at Maimonides Medical Center, the largest hospital in Brooklyn. Most of the other nurses were what they call "travelers" like them, filling shifts on the ward and ICU left open by the usual nurses who were out sick. Nearly all the patients in the hospital had COVID, with only one ward reserved for those who did not. The hospital modified many areas to fit in extra ICU beds for the surge. She immediately picked up four patients, three of whom were intubated. There was no time to contemplate the culture shock of the large orthodox Jewish community, or the big New York City hospital in general, coming from her small hospital. Everything was new to her, including the disease, which people still knew so little about. She had to be flexible, adapt quickly, listen, and figure things out. Not everyone is able to do this, but I had seen her succeed at this very thing 10 years prior at the ICU in Haiti.

The first night, as a colleague's patient became unstable, Portia asked: "Are they full code?" Portia wondered whether they should prepare to do CPR and call a "code blue," as would be standard protocol in this situation.

"No," replied the other nurse, one of the few long-term staffers working that night. "We don't do CPR on COVID patients at all."

"Really?" Portia asked, surprised. "Why not? Is it the lack of supplies?"

"We did do CPR at the beginning, but it never worked," she replied in a haggard voice. "Their lungs are done, so doing chest compressions on the heart, how is that going to help?"

Portia wondered at this response. Later, she noted the doctors did not seem to be in any rush to the bedside as the patients struggled. How much was that a different culture at the big New York hospital, and how much was learned helplessness in the face of the COVID onslaught? To watch people teeter towards death without calling for help, attempting lifesaving measures, or using the defibrillator was completely foreign to this seasoned RN—including in Haiti. But this became the standard of care during that time in New York, which they had to do for the healthcare system to function at all. Patient after patient died, night after night. In the end, over 20,000 people died of COVID in the city during 2020.[1]

Having a good friend working with her helped Portia during those difficult times. She felt it was the people she worked with closely who sustained her in such a frightening, stressful, horrible situation. In addition, New Yorkers came to their doors and windows at 7 PM every night to clap and sing thanks to the healthcare workers for their amazing work and sacrifice, a tradition that caught national attention.[2,3] Because of the night shifts, she was only able to experience this one time, when she opened her door at dusk one day to that hearty, earthy, visceral expression of gratitude that poured hope and energy into her soul.

For Portia, her time in New York was tough, but not nearly as hard on her as when COVID later came to her own town and her own hospital in Florida. Her New York experience was as an outsider: someone who could come in, help for a short time, and then leave that horror behind. Like many, she thought New York had the problem because so many people were packed together in one place. Surely the rest of the country would be spared.

Like most of us, Portia was still in denial. COVID did spread to the rest of the country. As the patients in her own ICU agonized, Portia suffered the emotional trauma of working in her now-expanded ICU over many months.

---

[1] Li W. et al., Summary of Vital Statistics 2020 (Bureau of Vital Statistics, New York City Department of Health and Mental Hygiene), accessed September 25, 2024, https://www.nyc.gov/assets/doh/downloads/pdf/vs/2020sum.pdf.

[2] Gary Hardcastle, "Every Night, New York Salutes its Health Care Workers," NPR, April 10, 2020, https://www.npr.org/2020/04/10/832131816/every-night-new-york-city-salutes-its-health-care-workers.

[3] Andy Newman, "What New York Sounds Like Every Night at 7," New York Times Web Video Interactive, accessed August 3, 2024, https://www.nytimes.com/interactive/2020/04/10/nyregion/nyc-7pm-cheer-thank-you-coronavirus.html. Note Mr. Newman points out that the tradition of cheering for the medical workers started in Wuhan, China.

As Portia cared for COVID patients in her hometown, it became more real to her because she identified much more with the patients. It wasn't just the elderly that she cared for: she remembers one mom in her 40s with preteens at home. After she died, the next patient to come into that ICU bed was another mom in her 40s. She too died. Her work was drastically different from her prior years of ICU work. Her colleagues leaned on gallows humor—as ICU nurses do—and told each other they were working in the "living morgue." The patients they treated for days and weeks died anyway.

The intensity of watching her patients die was compounded by having to tell their loved ones that the patient could not be saved. Though she had previously had these conversations as an ICU nurse, there were so many so often now that she felt an accumulation of emotion pushing her to the limit of her internal capacity. Most of the time, family members could not be present at the time of their loved one's passing.

Portia advised a woman with a BiPAP mask[1] on for her low oxygen levels: "You should talk to your family." The woman was so tired. She slowly reached for a pen—she didn't want to spend energy on speaking, which was so difficult. Portia patiently waited for her to scratch out the words. Some of them she had to ask her to write again. Finally, she understood that the patient had talked to her daughter on the phone a couple days ago, so she was OK, no need to call her again.

"What do you mean my mother is dead?" screamed the woman's 17-year-old daughter the next day when Portia called her. "The last time I heard, everything was fine, and she was getting better!" Portia heard the anger and gave what felt like lifeless words to a hopeless teen.

Another day, Portia had just sat down at the nurses' station to rest her aching legs. Next to her, a doctor was making a phone call. "Mrs. Green? This is Dr. Umbridge. I'm sorry to say, but your husband just died." There was a pause as the doctor listened. He looked over at Portia and raised his eyebrows as he said into the phone, "The nurse who took

---

[1] You can sometimes avoid full intubation using a tight-fitting face mask on the patient with the connected machine giving timed breathing support. This is called "BiPAP."

care of him is here, she can answer your questions." As he said this, the doctor deftly rose from his chair. He put the phone down in front of her as he made his quick exit.

"Hello?" said Portia, dizzy from the handoff, but trying to focus. "Mrs. Green?" She heard only hysterical crying. Sobbing that lasted a full 10 minutes.

"Portia?" Mrs. Green said finally. "Are you there?"

"I'm right here, honey, I'm right here."

"Can you stay on the line while I throw up?"

"You go right ahead," Portia said, "if that helps."

It was another half an hour of vomiting and crying before Mrs. Green was off the phone. That conversation still haunts Portia.

The next unexpected challenge was the reception Portia received from some of her previously supportive friends. When Portia got her COVID shot, she excitedly posted her vaccine card on Facebook. Later, her picture and vaccine card, with nasty comments, showed up on several anti-vax sites and Facebook pages. She and other friends tried to get the posts deleted, begging people to please take down her personal information, including her birth date. But they saw no problem with criticizing her and compromising her privacy.

Church was another big challenge. When Portia had gone to New York, Sunday school kids from her church had sent her cards of encouragement and support. But over time, extremism and denial took over. Masks were tolerated at first, but then scorned. Some members used the church as a platform to repeat misinformation they had heard online. One petite grandmother sick in the hospital with COVID told Portia she knew she got it from someone who knowingly came to church with COVID but no mask. She did not leave the hospital alive. Many people who should have been the most considerate proved to be the least caring.

"You people are exaggerating how bad the problem is," a church friend told Portia. She had never been a "you people" before. This kind, gentle, caring ICU nurse, with no time or energy for a life outside of the hospital amid the outbreak, who found solace and strength in the clapping of unknown New Yorkers, felt like a sinkhole had opened in her own town that might swallow her up.

"What's the matter, Mrs. Johnson?" Portia asked, seeing tears on her patient's face. "You're doing so much better—you will be leaving the ICU today."

"I really appreciate you, Portia," replied Mrs. Johnson. "Everyone has been so kind and loving and helpful. I owe you all so much."

"So it's only tears of joy?" asked Portia as she gathered her patient's belongings for the transfer. It always took extra energy to breathe through the N95 masks and have gloves and gown on for every little task.

"Well…I am also thinking about my friends from church. I was so short of breath, but they told me I mustn't go into the ER. 'They are only trying to make you sick and get your money,' they said." She looked out the window as some more tears came out. "I don't know why I listened to those friends. I'm sorry I doubted you. And I'm so glad I came in!" She turned back to Portia and her yellow getup, paused over her bed with her own tears behind her goggles, fogging them up.

Though she still wholeheartedly loves Jesus, because of the trauma, Portia has not felt safe returning to church since COVID. To avoid further wounds and polarizing conversations, she stopped talking to people about COVID outside of work. Though she had intended to continue in direct patient care, because of the toll the crisis had taken on her heart, Portia eventually moved to a non-clinical position. Nonetheless, she says, if faced with the same situation as in 2020, she would do it all again.

I was surprised and honored that Portia shared all those difficult experiences after we had not talked in more than 10 years. She had not discussed this much with anyone before, afraid to let the boxed-up feelings out, and was starting counseling to work on it. Portia remembered me talking to a young mother in the hospital courtyard in Haiti years ago who was suffering from domestic abuse. She recalled that I told the woman that she was worthy: that she did not deserve the abuse and was worth much, much more than this. Remembering those words, she felt she could trust me with her experiences. So, to Portia and all the other nurses who were on the front lines, I say: You are worthy also! You deserve thanks and honor, not the anger and vitriol that you received. God sees you! You are not invisible to him who sees all things and hears all that is spoken! God speaks to you as his angel spoke to Cornelius in Acts 10: "Your prayers have been heard, and your gifts to the poor have been noticed by God."[1]

---

[1] Acts 10:31 (NLT).

Chapter Six: Unemployed

There is a time for everything, and a season for every activity under the heavens.

— Ecclesiastes 3:1 (NIV)

There's a ton of untapped potential trapped under lame policies, poor direction, and stifling bureaucracies.

— Jason Fried & David Hansson[1]

I was still thinking about whether there was other public health work I could help with. The COVID wards were only the tip of the iceberg: what about where people caught it and transmitted it? That was outside the hospital doors. I brought up various ideas to other doctors and administrators but mostly got blank stares. What if we formed a group of people focused on creative solutions? Perhaps people who had seen different cultures and systems who could more easily imagine alternative approaches. Maybe even people outside of the medical system, who hadn't learned where the do-not-walk-here signs were. I thought of my friend Patrick Hastings: creative and capable but not in the medical field. Would he be willing to work with me? I could use my business, Bird's Eye Medical, which I had formed several years prior. I had used the company to help the new hospital in Elma, Washington, to

---

[1] Jason Fried and David Heinemeier Hansson, *Rework* (Crown Business, 2010), 253.

set up their inpatient work.[1] We could take a bird's eye view of the problem and target solutions from there. Or was I dreaming too big? Maybe I was overly proud, thinking that I could have some useful impact. My daughter thought I was going a little stir-crazy during lockdown, probably she was correct.

Jennifer and I had known Patrick for years through our church, Westwood Baptist, in Olympia. He did his pastoral internship as a youth leader at the church when David, our oldest son, was in the youth group. Patrick did a wonderful job at helping youth navigate tricky teen years, when they need a trusted adult leader who can guide without being overbearing, who can identify with them without getting lost in the teen drama. A positive influence in their lives besides parents and good peers.

After finishing a master of arts in international studies at Western Seminary in Portland, Patrick moved to China to pursue more academics. He first concentrated on improving his Chinese language with tutors and intensive self-study for about two years. Then he completed a two-year degree in management science at Xi'an Jiaotong University and went on to work in agriculture-related business. He became fluent in the Chinese language and well connected to the people of China. He fell in love with China and the Chinese people. In Xi'an he also fell in love with Krista, an American who had grown up in China, also fluent in Chinese.

When we visited China as a family around 2011, we spent a couple of weeks with Patrick, navigating the sunny island city of Xiamen where he was studying. We all did some Chinese language learning with his tutor, Tony. Later, our son David, inspired by his former youth leader, wound up spending a year in Xiamen after high school, focusing on his own Chinese language learning. On another trip, when a doctor friend and I went to Guizhou and met with local medical staff for an educational exchange, Patrick helped translate for us.

When Patrick and Krista got married in the States, we were excited

---

[1] Paul Bunge, "A Model for Internal Medicine Physicians in a Small Rural Hospital," *Rural and Remote Health* 18, no. 3 (2018), 4419, https://doi.org/10.22605/RRH4419.

to attend their wedding. Several years later we visited them in Xining on the border of the Tibetan plateau and saw his amazing work with greenhouses in that majestic, windswept place full of fascinating minority groups. We walked and prayed about their married life, their two girls, and the adoption of a boy from the local orphanage. We mourned and rejoiced with them when they moved back from China in August 2019 to set up their new home in Tacoma, Washington. They took a break after the whirlwind of adoption and moving, but by December, Patrick busied himself looking for work.

Patrick could make friends with anyone. He was the family peacekeeper growing up, a calming presence searching for compromise between sometimes warring siblings. In China, he was a natural salesman, making deals between an Israeli greenhouse company and local businesses and government officials. His network of connections seemed endless. One day during our visit there, we found ourselves volunteering to plant cherry trees in a Tibetan community. Good, hard, satisfying work.

With his remarkable talents and experience, we were surprised when Patrick couldn't find employment back in the States. With a business degree and experience working for the Murdock Trust, he applied with the Gates Foundation, as well as for several business positions. Employers weren't sure what to do with his overseas experience, with one master's earned in China and another from a seminary.

"How's the job applications?" I asked Patrick on the phone one day.

"It's slow," Patrick said, still somehow sounding positive. "But I made it to a second interview last week on Zoom."

"That's good, what happened?"

"Well, the guy asked lots of good questions, and we were talking about what the company does. It sounded like the kind of work I was doing with various businesses in China, connecting them, emphasizing sales, and the like. I told him that. But do you know what he said?"

"What?"

"He said their management team had talked about me, and I sounded like a purple chicken."

"A purple chicken, what does that have to do with anything?"

"He said everyone wants to have a look at me, but they are afraid of hiring me. They just don't know what I can do."

"Aw," I said, "sorry to hear that. Must be frustrating. You have had so many experiences that others have not had; in places they have never been. They can't see your value."

"It is getting old, I admit," Patrick replied, quick to add something positive, "but I have had plenty of time with the kids, and that is so important, especially time with the adopted one."

"You have amazing kids," I said, sad that we couldn't see them more often. "Listen Patrick, I have something to ask you. Feel completely free to say no. Please feel under no obligation. I have been thinking about doing more about the COVID pandemic, to see what we could put together to help with testing or education, like in churches. I have some experience and training in public health through the military and in Liberia. Probably this will wind up to be nothing, but it seems like there are so many things that could be done, and you are not working, maybe we could work together on this, but we would have to figure it out as we go."

"I'm very interested," Patrick said immediately. He wanted to help. He knew the problem was bad.

We talked over some more details and then I continued: "First, please talk it over with your wife and pray about it. Even before your story about the purple chicken, I was and I remain completely convinced that if they knew who you were and what you can do, you would have 10 job offers tomorrow. And if you get another job while we are trying to put things together, don't worry about it—you are free to do that."

Patrick did talk to his wife and pray, but from that moment he was committed. We started putting out feelers. Patrick talked to public health authorities in Pierce County where he lived to see if they needed help. I talked to Thurston County where I lived. I worked on possible methods for more sensitive testing for COVID-19 in hospitalized patients and talked to a patent lawyer. We looked at assisting at testing sites, and I signed up with laboratories and did some testing of homeless folks in our community. I volunteered with Medical Teams International, a group I had gone overseas with, as they turned their local mobile dental vans into portable COVID testing sites around the state. I found myself on the street outside homeless shelters in Seattle guiding people through nose swabs.

"There's a ventilator shortage, and I have a machine shop factory, what can we do?" It was my friend Norman Salmon. Norman has a fascinating company specializing in nanotechnology in Olympia.[1] Indeed he did have an assortment of machinery that could be turning out delicate parts for ventilators when New York was running out of them. Norman gets bored easily, and his machines were all idle several times during the pandemic shutdown.

It was a great question: could he make ventilators? Probably not per standard and quickly enough to make a difference by himself, but he could connect with a large hospital or university and contribute parts for locally adapted equipment. But after considering the question, I responded: "Norman, that is great that you want to help! That means so much! But I think by the time you got something going, it may not make much of a difference, since that is what everyone is working on right now. But you could certainly look at something else related to the pandemic, something others are not focused on but needs attention."

We talked about other equipment and about COVID overall for a while. I described one thing I had noticed: "The hospitals are short on disposable stethoscopes. We use those in the COVID rooms to help decrease transmission. They are very cheaply made and you can tell. Is there some way you could produce stethoscopes, perhaps a little better quality ones?"

Norman thought for a moment. "Maybe," he said. "What are the essentials?"

"Well, there are three parts as I understand it. The head of the stethoscope, that you put on the chest, is probably the most important, since it really must catch the sound. It is the head that gets fancier as the stethoscope gets more expensive and sounds better. The rest is just tubing and the earpieces. The tubing must be thick enough or it won't transmit the sound. And don't make the earpieces too small or they go way in your ears and hurt." It was a pretty simplistic description.

---

[1] Hummingbird Scientific, www.hummingbirdscientific.com.

With that and not much more, and input from his connections in India, his team created a disposable stethoscope that was mostly 3D printed within a week. I tried it out at the hospital, and it worked better than the ones they were running short on. Norman looked at ways to ramp up production.

Patrick and I considered other groups that we might help: dental offices and churches.

Dentists had closed their offices mid-March to save masks and reduce virus spread. How could we offer support as they prepared to reopen? I talked to a dentist friend many times about things like masking, HEPA filters, test kits, sick employees, and possible ways to reduce risk once they reopened. But despite multiple emails and phone calls, the other local dental offices ignored us. Finally, one staff member unleashed a long monologue on the phone that was quite enlightening. She explained, none too patiently, how their hygienists and others had for years tackled infection control issues from HIV to flu, and they certainly did not need a new fly-by-night doctor with no dental history to "help" them. Though my sensitivities were stepped on, it was good to know that most dentists were taking safety seriously. While I could tell they were not aware of everything we might have helped them with, that conversation helped us to focus our efforts elsewhere.

The other group we targeted was churches. We started with our own: Westwood Baptist. We would advise them and help them develop and implement plans, all without charging them. We could then use that experience to serve other churches. I envisioned lectures with groups of pastors, mass testing pre-church services, training videos, safe small group meetings while the big gatherings were suspended, and more.

The elders agreed to an assessment and an initial set of recommendations, but it quickly became clear that we had different goals. I envisioned creative discussions on how to maximize outreach and ministry while minimizing the risk of COVID transmission, infections, and death. The head elder told me he wanted all activities, from worship to Sunday school, exactly the way they were before COVID. He mostly just wanted to know the minimum legal requirements needed to remain open to the public and to stay out of trouble with the government. We had different agendas, and we were told they would not need our services.

Westwood's approach was common across the country, but not universal. On the other end of the safety spectrum was the local Chinese church we also attended. They asked my advice before I offered it, and I gave the congregation updates on COVID regularly. But the elders were resistant to a more nuanced approach, with small group meetings or meeting outside. They moved to Zoom services early on. People without good access to technology became disconnected. The church building stayed closed long after vaccines were widely available and other churches had reopened. Though I have since heard of many churches more creatively balancing safety precautions and the need for community, Patrick and I were not invited into that space. Our brief foray into trying to help churches on a larger scale went nowhere.

So, what next? As the first national wave tapered off, supply issues became much less urgent and the stethoscope project lost steam. The county health departments were catching up on their work and did not seem to need our help. Testing in our area was doing OK and the lines of cars at testing sites disappeared. We had tried several things, but none showed promise. Jennifer reminded me that I had said if nothing happened, I wouldn't just keep pouring time and money down the drain. Patrick and I agreed to put things on hold. He would continue looking for another job, and I would focus on my hospital work and the master's degree I was slowly working on at the seminary.

After the first wave of COVID, the second most interesting medical phenomenon of the decade, and possibly the century, occurred with no fanfare. The number of people being hospitalized dropped sharply, much more of a drop than can be explained by canceled elective surgeries and other COVID-related issues.[1,2] Some have theorized that less pollution made people healthier, with factories closed and people

[1] John Birkmeyer et al., "The Impact Of The COVID-19 Pandemic On Hospital Admissions In The United States," *Health Affairs* 39, no. 11 (2020), 2010–2017, https://doi.org/10.1377/hlthaff.2020.00980.
[2] Michael Reschen et al., "Impact of the COVID-19 pandemic on emergency department attendances and acute medical admissions," *BMC Emergency Medicine* 21, no. 143 (2021), https://doi.org/10.1186/s12873-021-00529-w.

driving less. Spending extra time with loved ones, walking more, and getting outside may have had a health benefit. Others suggested that fewer people were getting sick because there was less sharing of the usual viruses and other contagions that we pass to each other every day. I think this last theory holds a lot of weight. I suspect that we as a medical community, and society at large, vastly underestimate the damage that viruses in general cause. They probably contribute much more than we give them credit for to heart attacks, strokes, and the like, as well as the respiratory problems we commonly think of. We may have missed a unique opportunity to study this issue, focused as we all were on one single virus.

Whatever the reasons for fewer patients, the hospitals cut their teams, and per diem workers like myself were the first to lose shifts. Our business startup had gone nowhere. The hospitals didn't have consistent work for me. Now I was mostly unemployed, too!

But back in Canada, Mom needed my help.

Chapter Seven:
What Canada Taught Me About COVID

The sea gave up its dead, and death and the grave gave up their dead. And all were judged according to their deeds.
– Revelation 20:13 (NLT)

But in the end, it has been the inconveniences that have mattered to me the most.
– Amor Towles[1]

J ennifer and I looked into moving closer to Canada since my mother was still at my sister Sarah's house right across the border near Vancouver, BC. Sarah and her husband decided they couldn't subject Mom to the endless COVID lockdowns and risks at a nursing facility. So many people couldn't visit with their families or were limited to waving through the windows, not to mention the risk of getting COVID seemed highest there. So, they kept Mom with them, squeezing together to make it work. But the bulk of her belongings were still in her condo she owned in Edmonton. We had left her things behind in our haste to move her and get home, which turned out to be just before lockdowns.

---

[1] The main character, Alexander Rostov, reflects on his life in the novel: Amor Towles, A Gentleman in Moscow (Penguin Books, 2016), 352.

Mom's stuff and her condo needed attention. It had been months since we had been there, and it was a burden on her neighbor to check on the place. I blocked off time from work, as COVID cases were down that summer. Jennifer and I flew to Edmonton in July after we outlined our COVID prevention plan for the Alberta Health Authority. We experienced firsthand Canada's more stringent and coordinated approach to the virus. We stayed at my mother's house for the required two-week quarantine, since it was empty anyway, sorting and packing her things. The local public health department checked on us to make sure we were following the plan, and we were tested preventatively. Mom's church friends left groceries, boxes, and other supplies on the porch, no one expecting to interact. My other sister, also named Jennifer, joined us from Colorado with her two daughters.

It was a combined packing exercise, mini-reunion, and isolation pod. My mother does not like to throw things away, so we had quite the task of sorting her stuff into three groups: one to ship to British Columbia, one to give away to the thrift stores, with the rest allocated to the landfill. We made music, my artistic sister drew, and we played games to fill up the non-packing time. At night, the coyotes in the field behind my mom's fence howled mournfully. We finished the job just before the two weeks ended. Though it was painful to throw away mementos, the group had a wonderful time together. My nieces and I used leftover packing materials along with odds and ends to make a monstrous marble run, which started on the roof and meandered noisily into the backyard.

Once out of quarantine and still healthy, we worked to get the appropriate things to the thrift stores and the house ready for sale. A helpful realtor and others helped us to pull it off all in one trip, which was good since the border remained very difficult to cross for months to come.

After we finished up the plans with the realtor and the moving company, my wife and I drove Mom's car over the mountains to Vancouver to sell. The only challenge with that leg of the trip was the lodging in the mountains between Alberta and BC. Amazingly picturesque, Banff, Alberta, and the surrounding area had become a popular place for isolation-frustrated and work-at-home Americans to escape to, despite the Canadian restrictions. A trick I heard was to tell the Canadian border guards that you were on your way to Alaska, and then just drive to Banff. By the time we arrived at our hotel, the Canadians were on to this charade and had sent several people packing. When they saw our US identification, the hotel staff immediately turned angry and accusatory. In vain, we explained our story and how we were just trying to get the car to BC. We were likely the least infectious people in town after two weeks in quarantine but were viewed as irresponsible and asked to restrict ourselves to our room and instant ramen.

Despite our frustration in Banff, I noticed that the Canadian approach surprisingly led to a kind of increase in freedom and social connections. Many Canadians were still frustrated, as illustrated later by a movement led by long-haul truckers protesting restrictions.[1] And I truly feel for those who were stuck for so long without their usual connections and limited work. However, with the Canadian public health approach more focused on limiting travel and large group gatherings, they had fewer cases of COVID, and people could gather in smaller groups, such as with families and friends, with less risk. I saw fewer people wearing masks, which was possible because the big-picture tasks of tracking cases and limiting cross-province travel were more effectively implemented. Paradoxically, the more stringent restrictions gave Canadians more freedom to get together locally, while also saving lives. I wonder if their mental health was better served as well, as they were not forced into the unsolvable problem of being individually responsible for the success or failure of public health.

Did Canada's more proactive approach make a measurable difference? The death rate from COVID overall per one million population in the US through March 2023 was approximately 3,331. The rate in New Zealand, one of the developed countries most successful in limiting COVID-related deaths, was only 642. Canada, though, is more like the United States—less geographically isolated

---

[1] "The convoy crisis in Ottawa: A timeline of key events," CBC, February 17, 2022, https://www.cbc.ca/news/canada/ottawa/timeline-of-convoy-protest-in-ottawa-1.6351432.

than New Zealand, with many similarities to the US in terms of language, comparable healthcare access, geographical size, and varied population. Canada made and enforced several specific public health decisions that were different than those made in the US during the pandemic which would explain a lower death rate. As of March 2023, Canada lost 1,350 per million population to COVID. If the US had taken similar steps and achieved the reduction in deaths achieved by Canada, then instead of about 1.1 million COVID deaths in the US, there would have been about 450,000 deaths. As many as 650,000 American lives could have been saved.[1] If this estimate is accurate even within several hundred thousand, it is staggering. There is no way now to bring these people back. But reflecting on what our country could have done better is very important if we want to be people who learn, who want to improve, and who care about the future.

Sociologist Jarome Karabel, in a well-written Time Magazine article, calculated a similar number of American lives that could have been saved and notes that the difference in death rate likely had many causes, including Americans being less healthy overall, and America's "powerful strand of libertarianism at odds with the individual sacrifices necessary for the common good."[2]

Early on in the pandemic, a doctor friend of mine traveled to another state, where the local public health authority told her to restrict herself to her house and direct family for two weeks. She laughed as she told me how she ignored this directive and took her kids all over the place, visiting and enjoying the sites. When local public health called and visited the house, to avoid repercussions, she made up some story about why they were not home. I doubt many Canadian doctors did the same.

I recall watching the news as COVID spread on cruise ships in

---

[1] The population of the US in March of 2023 (the same time as the Johns Hopkins data) was 335,417,284 as estimated by the US census bureau (https://www.census.gov/popclock/). Using the per population number from Canada, the estimated US death rate could have been: $334,417,284/100,000 \times 135 = 451,463$.

[2] Jerome Karabel, "The U.S. Failed Miserably on COVID-19. Canada Shows it Didn't Have to Be That Way," *Time*, May 23, 2022, https://time.com/6180309/covid-19-us-canada-differences.

March of 2020. Those on board were stuck at sea as ports blocked them, and many of the passengers and crew became sick. Plans for quarantine, isolation, and strategies for testing were hit and miss. One of our sick COVID hospital patients was one of these passengers. She reported getting off a cruise ship in Florida feeling ill, and then immediately taking a commercial flight to Seattle. When I heard that story, I feared our country was not going to seriously implement the needed travel restrictions. Canada, however, took all of these issues, including the cruise ship cases, much more seriously.[1]

Another major cultural difference between the US and Canada was the superstar status of the provincial public health authorities. Most of our British Columbia relatives still talk fondly of "Dr. Bonnie," the BC Public Health Officer during COVID. As Dr. Bonnie Henry regularly updated them on the progress of the pandemic, people would track these numbers as if they were as important as their hockey team's rankings. Dr. Bonnie was featured in a New York Times article[2] and has her own Wikipedia entry.[3]

In contrast to the Canadian doctors, struggling public health doctors in the US were threatened, limited, heckled, and in some cases fired outright.[4] Later in the pandemic, I worked with Dr. Bob Lutz, an extremely capable and intelligent public health doctor. He had been working hard fighting COVID as county health officer in Washington State's second-largest city, Spokane. In October 2020, a senior administrator showed up with a security guard and said, "Dr. Lutz, please put your work keys, laptop, and cell phone on the table." Then he

---

[1] "Canada to repatriate citizens on coronavirus-hit cruise ship in California," CBC, March 8, 2020, https://www.cbc.ca/news/world/covid-19-coronavirus-march-8-1.5490199.

[2] Catherine Porter, "The Top Doctor Who Aced the Coronavirus Test," *New York Times*, June 5, 2020, https://www.nytimes.com/2020/06/05/world/canada/bonnie-henry-british-columbia-coronavirus.html.

[3] "Bonnie Henry," *Wikipedia, The Free Encyclopedia*, last modified November 5, 2024, https://en.wikipedia.org/wiki/Bonnie_Henry.

[4] Anna King, "Embattled Public Health Workers Leaving At 'Steady And Alarming Rate,'" NPR, November 25, 2020, https://www.npr.org/2020/11/25/938873547/embattled-public-health-workers-leaving-at-steady-and-alarming-rate.

was escorted out of the building.[1] Not quite superstar status.

After returning to Washington State, I got busy back at the hospitals, which again needed more help. The summer lull was over and the wards were again filling up with COVID patients. At the same time, I started getting responses to job applications I had put out when work was slow, so I did virtual interviews for jobs in Olympia as well as up north, closer to Canada. We put money down for a house still to be built near the border in Ferndale, Washington. I hoped and prayed I was wrong about COVID and it would soon calm down. Borders had to get back to normal soon. For now, the best we could do to see family was sit along corresponding farm roads on the US-Canada line and shout at each other over the ditch, hoping my mother and her walker would not slip while cars whizzed by behind them. One time it was so cold and windy, I am not sure we caught a single full sentence from each other before rushing back to the cars to warm up.

My frustration with inconsistent work, no openings up north, and challenges in crossing the border led us to decide to accept a half-time slot with Providence Hospice in Olympia. We could put the Ferndale house up for rent once it was built. For now, we would continue the across-ditch visits with Mom. And I would keep working at the hospitals when they needed me, which was plenty in the fall of 2020. I started with hospice in November.

Patrick periodically gave me updates about possible COVID work outside of the hospitals from the many inquiries that he had made. The updates consisted of him saying nobody had called. I still felt useful in caring for people at the hospitals, though I remained frustrated with systemic issues I could not change.

With my prior volunteer connections, I continued to try to be a resource and gave some lectures on Zoom. I answered questions that came from the jungles of Southeast Asia about oxygen strategies, proning, and protective gear. I continued my slow journey through my

---

[1] Adam Shanks and Arielle Dreher, "Former Spokane County Health Officer Bob Lutz was fired illegally, preliminary state investigation concludes," *The Spokesman-Review*, May 12, 2021, https://www.spokesman.com/stories/2021/may/12/preliminary-investigation-health-district-administ/.

master's degree. My remote professor didn't answer emails for weeks, and later discussions confirmed he had been hospitalized with COVID, but thankfully recovered.

I felt like I was back in the military: watching casualty statistics, treating the patients who came in injured, but unable to change things like stopping the US from invading Iraq or preventing people from making Improvised Explosive Devices (IEDs). Just as I had watched the creeping rise in the numbers of military personnel lost, I now watched the statistics as thousands, then tens of thousands, then hundreds of thousands of Americans died of COVID-19. The most useful measure for tracking the progress of the virus and our fight against it was the morbid deaths-per-day number.

Maybe it's because I lost my father at an early age, but one thing that infuriates me is when people die when they do not need to. When someone dies from something so preventable, like drunk driving, or a five-year-old kid accidentally shooting his sister with the unlocked handgun he found around the house, I get angry. It feels like someone is laughing at my own loss, like they are saying, "We don't care that your dad died of cancer; death doesn't really matter. If it did, I would have put on my seatbelt instead of crashing without it." It throws my grief in my face like a bucket of water, leaving me breathless and sputtering. Maybe that's why I am still angry at people who did not take COVID precautions seriously. I am still trying to catch my breath. I know I need to be an adult and accept other people's decisions and opinions, but I struggle. I also know I need to forgive, but how do you forgive people for over half a million needless deaths? In some ways, I wish I didn't know about these realities of COVID. Better to build marble runs, go to Banff, watch TikTok, and not think.

Then Pierce County called.

Chapter Eight: Pierce County

*And Elisha prayed, "Open his eyes, L*ORD*, so that he may see." Then the L*ORD *opened the servant's eyes, and he looked and saw the hills full of horses and chariots of fire all around Elisha.*
— 2 Kings 6:17 (NIV)

The greatness of a community is most accurately measured by the compassionate actions of its members.
— Coretta Scott King[1]

P ierce is a large county, a mix of urban (Tacoma) and rural areas. The western part of the county includes a section of scenic Puget Sound, including many inlets and several small islands. The current Tacoma Narrows bridge replaced the one that collapsed famously in 1940. Many a high school science class has viewed footage of the poorly planned bridge, nicknamed "Galloping Gertie" because it often oscillated in the wind, and the video shows a particularly windy day when it vibrated like a guitar string until it broke apart and fell into the gorge below.[2]

---

[1] Associated Press, "King's Widow Urges Acts of Compassion," *Los Angeles Times*, January 17, 2000.
[2] "Lessons from the failure of a great machine," Washington State Department of Transportation, accessed March 28, 2024, https://wsdot.wa.gov/TNBhistory/bridges-failure.htm.

Tacoma is a port city. From the port area and its mills and refinery arises a sulfur smell that passersby know lovingly as the "Tacoma aroma."[1] Tacoma is the home of the Museum of Glass where I once watched famous glass artist Dale Chihuly roughly directing a crew of glassblowers as they formed the most amazing pieces. Downtown has seen better times as well as worse times. Majestic church buildings and mansions suggest a booming port past.

Tacoma is the center of Washington State's African American population, which makes up 11% of the city, whereas statewide, the percentage of African Americans is only 4.6%.[2] Another 13% of Tacoma residents identify as "two or more races," also high for the state. The city also has large communities of Korean and Pacific Island descent.

To the east are suburbs, including Puyallup, home of the state fairgrounds. South of Tacoma is a large military base that includes an Air Force airport and an Army hospital. Further east, the county rises to Washington's largest peak, Mount Rainier, the most prominent summit[3] in the contiguous United States. The people of Seattle and Tacoma feel a sense of majesty and grounding when they see it. Despite its benevolent appearance, it is still an active volcano and could spell doomsday for many were it to lose its cool.

I completed my medical internship in 1995 at Madigan Army Medical Center in Pierce County. During that year, I tried to stop at the window every day to see what the mountain was up to. Sometimes it was shy, hiding in the winter clouds and rain. Often in the morning sunrise (I was almost always at the hospital before sunrise), orange and

---

[1] "Aroma of Tacoma," *Wikipedia, The Free Encyclopedia*, last modified August 13, 2024,https://en.wikipedia.org/w/index.php?title=Aroma_of_ Tacoma&oldid=1240160690.

[2] "Quickfacts," US Census Bureau, accessed March 28, 2024, https://www.census. gov/quickfacts.

[3] "Most Prominent," meaning it has the largest difference in elevation change between its base and its peak. "List of the highest major summits of the United States," *Wikipedia, The Free Encyclopedia*, last modified October 6, 2024, https://en. wikipedia.org/w/index.php?title=List_of_the_highest_major_summits_of_the_ United_States&oldid=1249796409.

red graced its slopes, while a persistent white cloud hid the mountain's top as if to say the clouds never completely loosen their grip on our corner of the world. That year was my first working completely at a military hospital, and it involved a steep learning curve of mostly medical knowledge, with a couple of weeks spent in tents in Texas for combat casualty care. I learned to respect the ICU nurses, survived cardiology sleep deprivation, and was extremely thankful when our first son, David, born at Madigan, was able to transfer out of the neonatal intensive care unit after a C-section, fever, and a wrestling match with high bilirubin. Years later, in 2008, I came back to Madigan as a civilian doctor and worked for nine years as a physician and teacher for the same training program. I look back fondly on my time there and the privilege of serving the military members and their families.

In October 2020, Ellen Lenk from the Pierce County Department of Emergency Management called us. Patrick had made several contacts there, and when they wanted to do a drive-through flu vaccination campaign, they thought of my company, Bird's Eye Medical. They needed nurses to give influenza shots.

I was not excited. I wanted to fight COVID. The US did not have a COVID vaccine yet. Masks, education, outreach, inventions: those were the things I wanted to do, not flu shots. How useful would flu shots be anyway, with so many people working from home and many schools still closed? Besides, I had just spent so many days during September in the hospital working: I was tired. Our two boys were home from college and work, studying and working remotely, and I was happy to spend any spare time I had with them, as we periodically rearranged one of the rooms upstairs with different themes as if we were going to various coffee shops. I still volunteered to do COVID testing with Medical Teams International—that seemed more COVID-related at least. The hospice job was to start in November: regular work that was not subject to hospital surge numbers, which also meant we would have medical insurance again.

But Patrick convinced me, salesman that he is. Why not get involved? Might turn into something more later. This county seemed to be proactive and effective, with plenty of expertise between the Emergency Management Department and the Tacoma-Pierce County

Health Department. It sounded like a small project that shouldn't take too much time and effort. We would only have to do the recruiting and hiring. Was that ever an understatement!

I started calling medical friends, an advantage of having worked in several hospitals and clinics over the years. I just wanted nurses to give flu shots. My ignorance helped. Had I known how much work was involved in payroll, HR, state and federal rules, contracts, insurance, and everything else, I would have said no. But saying yes was what trained us in these things, and so much more.

Pierce County used the flu shots exercise for two purposes: first, to get flu shots out so people and hospitals would be less likely to have yet another viral respiratory disease to deal with this season. Second, to practice mass vaccination drive-throughs with multiple agencies, contractors, and volunteers. They hoped the COVID shot was coming and knew the regular medical system would need to be supplemented. This was a dress rehearsal.

Their original plan was to use MultiCare nurses as the main workhorse vaccinators in the flu shot outreach. MultiCare is one of the large nonprofit hospital systems in the area. It currently boasts 12 hospitals and over 300 primary and specialty care clinics.[1] I remember asking Patrick why Pierce County wanted us to help get nurses, since the newspaper already had flyers for the flu events with the MultiCare logo. But I was not surprised that they were having difficulty: the hospitals were busy, hospital nurses are highly paid, and these large bureaucratic organizations are not the local, helpful nonprofits they used to be. I had my own theories on how unwieldy and overpriced our large health systems are, but I remembered how un-useful my strong opinions were during our church project. The best course for me would be to keep my mouth shut and focus on being helpful instead of sharing my views on how the medical system is broken. At the same time, I wanted to remember two realities as we did our own work: first, medical personnel are paid very handsomely in this country, one could argue too

[1] "About Us," MultiCare website, accessed February 5, 2024, https://www.multicare.org/about/.

handsomely; second, public health departments lack authority. If these two factors were hindering the medical system's capacity to give out flu shots and we wanted to be helpful, our strategy would have to take them into account.

I can see now what we could not then. If we had become busy with churches and dental offices, we would not have been able to say yes to Pierce County. We would have been too busy arguing with people and reinterpreting government directives as part of a complex game with no winners. Our frustration with how life is going often reflects our limited perspective on what God is up to.

We contracted with Pierce County to supply qualified personnel to give flu shots at urban and rural locations around the county in October and November of 2020. A wet, windy, relatively miserable enterprise. A prelude to many days of the same. Many months of the same.

We looked for registered nurses, licensed practical nurses, and medical assistants. We called and advertised and begged. We thought getting 13 vaccinators would be a challenge, and it was. But somehow, we had over 10 on that first rainy day. I learned more about vaccine logistics, supply chains, how to do medical work outdoors, how to keep people warm, and how to manage side effects in the field. Patrick conversed cordially with nurses, managers, ambulance drivers, and anyone else who had a minute to chat. He learned the nuances of county contracting, how nurses felt, and the writing and rewriting of contract proposals. We were in the mix with another small staffing company and one national one. We showed our ability to get staff working quickly and safely. But would this translate into meaningful COVID fighting work, or were we just going to be flu shot helpers?

"Dad, can I ask you something?" my son Nathan asked me one day. "When do you think I will be able to go back to college?" It was a treasure for Jennifer and me when the kids were home, but it was as if their lives were paused. Nathan chose Washington State University partly to join the marching band, and Zoom drumming was understandably dreadful.

I sketched out some simple math and graphs to show Nathan the problem. "As you can see here, COVID is on track to kill at least 1% of those who catch it; even up to 3%, depending on how good your medical care is, and whether your hospital is overwhelmed at the time with a surge in the area. So far, less than half of those people have died. That is why public health measures are still in place, to the degree that people and politics tolerate them." In the process of explaining the situation to my son, I was putting into words the conundrum that had been circling in my mind. I was facing my greatest pain: people dying.

"Either way," I continued, looking up from my sketch at Nathan, "people are still getting first-time COVID. On the one hand, slowly with restrictions; on the other hand, more quickly without them. Neither option is good!" I paused to think through my next point. "The only ways that I can see that might lead the country down a different path would be the development of an effective vaccine, or a dramatic change in COVID itself, a genetic shift that makes it much less dangerous."

"Well, are those things going to happen?" asked Nathan, frustrated.

"I don't know," I replied honestly. "I just don't know."

It was a depressing conversation. No wonder I had been loath to spell it out before, even to myself. What we didn't know at the time was that within one year, both would come to pass: we would have a quality vaccine available in America, and the dominant strain would change dramatically. Would those things truly save lives? And how much more social, political, and emotional damage would occur while we waited?

Nathan walked out of the room with a sad face. The restrictions were saving lives, but they brought hardships to so many, sometimes with deadly consequences, even an increase in suicides. And the sacrifices that young people made were in a way more difficult since the disease did not affect them as much as older folks.

In the meantime, it was time to get busy.

Chapter Nine: Testing and Nurturing

She opens her arms to the poor and extends her hands to the needy.
— Proverbs 31:20 (NIV)[1]

If you plant something and it doesn't grow, plant something else.
— Dip Singh[2]

"Patrick, I need to talk to you." It was Ellen Lenk. She, along with Trent Stephens, whom she had borrowed from the sheriff's department, were our main contacts in Pierce County.

"Ellen, good to see you, how are things?" asked Patrick, trying as usual to be friendly.

"Things are a load of shit, what else do you want to know?" Ellen said crisply. Colorful language was natural for Ellen from a young age. She grew up on Army bases until her father retired from the Army when she was 18. She herself dove into the world of rescues and ambulances. She had been with Pierce County's Department of Emergency Management (DEM) for 17 years.

"Listen, Patrick," Ellen said, asserting her authority and updating this young businessman who needed to be watched but seemed so

---

[1] Part of King Lemuel's extended description of a worthy, admirable woman: nurturing, hard working, strong, God fearing, and wise.

[2] Our neighbor who always has a great garden, talking about his experience with farming and gardening in India and the US.

capable. "I am the finance division manager for DEM. When COVID hit, so many other leaders left, and I picked up their jobs, too. I am busy, I am stressed, and I am trying to save lives. I need your help, and I need you to focus."

"Ellen, we are here to fight COVID. You tell us what we can do to help, and that's what we will do." Patrick and I talked over and over about this. We wanted to be available and do what was needed. If it was medically useful, and somebody else couldn't or wouldn't do it, we would try our very best to say yes.

"Fine, whatever, you did some flu shot clinics, good. Now get some more staff and help out with this school project. Don't talk to me until you have the paperwork all done." Ellen picked up the phone. "Trent, why aren't you in here yet? I'm way done with Patrick already."

Patrick took the cue and rushed out. He didn't particularly like wandering around emergency management; the culture and language were rough. But to do what was needed, he had to be available and aware, as the pieces moved quickly. He knew Ellen had a good heart, as well as a soft side. But when she needed to be a hammer, she didn't hesitate.

Along with one or two flu shot events each week, we were to supply nurses and administrative workers to do COVID testing at schools. The idea was to identify COVID-infected students and staff before they were symptomatic through weekly testing. With the push to reopen schools, officials juggled politics, safety, parental concerns, and the limitations of remote learning. If early infections were caught and people stayed home, maybe the spread would be reduced in the schools and the entire community. Rapid tests were now available, but it was hard to get access to them, and they were not yet over the counter. The requirement was that a medically trained person had to run the test.

For this project, we needed people who could work full time, but temporarily. All needed to be vetted for work with children. It was no surprise the government asked us for help: it takes time to start people working as government employees. The job-search website indeed.com seemed perfectly geared for us, unlike some other sites catering to large companies. It was as simple as posting an ad and waiting for someone to apply. Our workload was growing, and we needed help: recruiting, orienting, training, managing, and nurturing staff.

I immediately thought of Roberta Herrera. I had worked with Roberta at the Group Health clinic where she worked as an LPN (licensed practical nurse) for 11 years.[1] Roberta grew up in southern California, with plenty of Latino culture influence, and had a strong Catholic faith. She nurtured her family and others, including two boys, her son's friends, who later worked for us: Brian and Carlin. These two were often found at her house throughout their high school years and later, even after Roberta's son left for college.

Roberta would show up at the Group Health clinic every morning with her infectious smile, arms often full of savory flavors from south of the border. She overflowed with help and service for patients and staff, especially those who needed that extra encouragement to get better, to keep working, to get out of a hole. She was oil to the medical machine, keeping doctors and support staff at their best, which then brought the best to the patients.

Roberta had left Group Health to help care for her grandchildren, but I guessed that since they were now older, she might have space for more work.

"Hello, Dr. Bunge," Roberta said knowingly when she picked up the phone. I had called the clinic where we had both worked to find her number, and I was startled that she knew it was me, and she did not seem surprised.

"Hello, Roberta. So good to hear your voice! How's the grandbabies?" I asked.

"They are good, trying to make it through COVID. Everyone healthy right now."

After some more catching up, I said, "Roberta, feel free to say no, but I wanted to tell you what I am up to and see if you would consider being a part of it." I told her about Bird's Eye Medical and the things we were up to with flu shots and the upcoming school project. I had plenty more to say when she interrupted me:

"Of course I'll help you, Dr. Bunge."

---

[1] Kaiser Permanente took over Group Health soon after she left.

I wasn't sure what to say next. "Do you want to check with your husband first? This position could be a lot of work and then not stay stable…"

"No problem, Dr. Bunge. If you are doing something about COVID, it must be good, and I want to get on board." I felt humbled and blessed at that moment that such a wise nurse was ready to trust me that much. I knew that came with a big responsibility as well.

"Roberta, are you sure this is the first time you heard about this?" I asked.

"Well, staff at the office might have given me a heads-up."

I remembered how close Roberta was to all the clinic staff. They must have called to tell her I was looking for her. She was ready for action, which was good because there was loads of work to do.

We verified the staff's licensing and training, and Pierce County expertly provided further on-site training and supervision. Jennifer, Patrick, Roberta, and I called potential workers every night. Jennifer and I worked long hours, trying to maximize daylight hours for talking to potential employees, troubleshooting, and my hospice work. Early mornings and late evenings were emails, government paperwork, finance decisions, business plans, and hospice paperwork. It takes a lot to add employees to your company.

I made sure that during our interview process, all the employees clearly understood that despite our strict use of protective measures, they were at risk of getting COVID at the schools. Most of the applicants turned out to be younger, but there were a few who were not young at all, and I worried more about them. But they clearly knew their risks and wanted to help. Soon, we had teams doing testing at 10 schools around the county.

The county health department tracked the schools and their infection rates. The data suggested that our work with screening did lessen the risk of outbreaks. This added to data from other parts of the country suggesting that, yes, regular screening with rapid tests at schools was useful to cut down the spread of COVID in the whole community. But beyond pilot projects like ours, the school testing did not seem to gain much traction around the country. It was difficult for people to see how testing kids and making them miss more school when they didn't feel sick was worth it, especially when COVID wasn't as bad in kids.

In November 2020, more than 1,000 Americans were dying every day from COVID. Like most, I did the job in front of me but carried this number like a heavy weight on my back. I answered phone calls from my hospice nurses and learned so much from the more experienced palliative care specialists I worked with. I still worked at the hospitals, knowing 1,000 deaths per day also meant countless others hospitalized who would recover. I stopped by the schools when I had time to check the lineup of cute little children as they were instructed in nose swabbing. (It made me sad to watch them swab, but at the same time it was obvious that kindergartners are not at all bothered by sticking something in their nose.) For my master's class, I wrote papers on race and counseling across cultures, though for the first time I was late turning in a paper. Was I trying to do too much? We devised training and updates for our employees. Jennifer and I tried to hike when we could. The rain can't stop you from going outside if you live in Western Washington—you must push through or you won't breathe fresh air all winter.

In early December, a missionary in the Philippines called asking questions about how to manage the COVID outbreak in their youth housing center. I was able to walk her through this but realized I also could use expert advice if I was going to run a COVID-fighting company. Dr. David Brett-Major had been the main instructor among many prominent specialists at the military's tropical disease course I had attended in 2009. Some Google searching showed not only was he now professor of infectious disease and public health at the University of Nebraska, he also had done crucial work with the World Health Organization during the 2013–2016 Ebola outbreak in West Africa. He put his life on the line seeing numerous Ebola patients and helped prevent that outbreak from spreading even further than the three overwhelmed countries. Like many heroes, he did not blow his own horn.[1]

---

[1] Dr. David Brett-Major was assigned by the US Navy to the WHO during the Ebola outbreak. He was in West Africa for many months in several locations. When Ebola threatened Nigeria, Africa's most populous nation, Dr. Brett-Major went there and

Dr. Brett-Major agreed to be a resource for me when I otherwise could not find answers, which was very helpful when I reached out later. He was involved in a similar school testing project to ours[1] and by the time I called him had already published several papers about COVID in the medical literature.[2] Once again, Dr. Brett-Major was a hero in a war without bullets.

In our Pierce County work giving flu shots, testing, and preparing for mass vaccinations, we were gaining experience and getting smarter. We developed a team of motivated workers we trusted, both nurses and clerical workers. My wife, Jennifer, handled the money. I poured into my hospice work—it was emotionally tough but fulfilling and interesting. I signed up for my next master's class at the university with more papers to write.

Then Lewis County called.

---

was crucial to their effective response, in partnership with Nigeria's public health departments. However, his recognition by the Navy was minimal, and the reports below from Scientific American and the WHO don't even mention him. But his own book and the Nigerian movie below tell the story.

Katherine Harmon Courage, "How Did Nigeria Quash Its Ebola Outbreak So Quickly?" *Scientific American*, October 18, 2014, https://www.scientificamerican. com/article/how-did-nigeria-quash-its-ebola-outbreak-so-quickly/.

WHO/A. Esiebo, "Successful Ebola responses in Nigeria, Senegal and Mali," *World Health Organization*, January 2015, https://www.who.int/news-room/ spotlight/one-year-into-the-ebola-epidemic/successful-ebola-responses-in-nigeria-senegal-and-mali.

David Brett-Major, *A Year of Ebola: A Personal Tale of the Weirdness Wrought by the World's Largest Ebola Virus Epidemic* (Navigating Health Risks, 2017).

93 Days, directed by Steve Gukas (Native Filmworks, 2016), 1:58, https://www. imdb.com/title/tt5305246/. Note Dr. Brett-Major was played by Scottish Actor Alastair Mackenzie.

[1] John Crowe et al. (including David Brett-Major), "Assessment of a Program for SARS-CoV-2 Screening and Environmental Monitoring in an Urban Public School District," *JAMA Network Open* 4, no. 9 (2021), https://doi.org/10.1001/ jamanetworkopen.2021.26447.

[2] Example and description of some of their work: David Brett-Major et al., "Advanced Preparation Makes Research in Emergencies and Isolation Care Possible: The Case of Novel Coronavirus Disease (COVID-19)," *American Journal of Tropical Medicine and Hygiene*, 102, no. 5 (2020): 926–931, https://www.doi. org/10.4269/ajtmh.20-0205.

Chapter Ten: Lewis County

Those who answer before they listen are foolish and disgraceful.
— Proverbs 18:13 (CEB)

The virtue of humility...is a far more precious treasure than all academic progress.
— Simon Weil[1]

L ewis County is mostly rural. Twin towns Centralia and Chehalis, along Interstate Highway 5 (I-5), contain the county's main hospital, a Walmart, an outlet mall, a bunch of churches, rival football teams, and a strong local culture. The county has a concentration of politically conservative, loud of mouth yet mostly lovable, usually flexible, white-shaded people.[2] The county extends west as rural rolling hills and farmland, with areas prone to flooding. The east of the county rises up between the majestic peaks of Mount Rainier and Mount St. Helens. St. Helens is the volcano that massively blew its benign-appearing top in 1980, destroying homes and highways, killing 57 people, and blasting ash for thousands of miles. My grandparents collected the grey-black

---

[1] Simon Weil, "Reflections On The Right Use Of School Studies With A View To The Love Of God," in *Waiting for God* trans. Emma Craufurd (HarperCollins, 2009).
[2] Like the rest of the American West, ancient peoples such as the Chehalis and Meshall, with rich traditions and long histories, populated the area prior to devastating diseases, encroachment, and treaties.

soot in Idaho, and I recall seeing the odd grey sky for several days as a teenager in Moosehorn, Manitoba, 1,500 miles away!

Lewis County takes your breath away with its mountain peaks, calming lakes, rolling farmland, alpine meadows, isolated valleys, tulip farms, and fantastic skiing at the pass between mountains. Yet with all its resources and beauty, county income lags, a large aging population struggles to access care, and a drug crisis saps joy and years.

JP Anderson had been Lewis County public health director only three months when the news about a new coronavirus in China broke. JP watched the news closely, and when a case showed up in the US, he went a little manic. He stayed up late and rose early outlining response plans and strategizing his incident command center. His energetic concern was not appreciated by some county officials who felt that a bunch of hype about a cold virus would not need that much attention.

At first, JP needed to hear the calming words of those who refused to get riled up by CNN predictions. In an emergency, we need people who, even if they don't have all the answers, can speak in a way that soothes the anxious soul. From my time working at military hospitals, I remember long speeches of controversy-avoidant leaders, expected to speak while avoiding any topic that might be remotely interesting. After the attacks of September 11, 2001, we craved that reassuring drone. It said to your panicking soul: Not everything is at risk. There is still plenty of boring stability here.

As the pandemic descended on Lewis County in particular, JP became one of those soothing voices himself as he was thrust into the role of spokesperson. Yet he retained the tenacity needed for the fights over masking, school closures, stay-at-home advice, and the rest. County leaders made provocative public statements, at times arguing against public health directives. But behind closed doors, JP found that together they could strike a balance for the county. During those months, he learned the value of working quickly, with a sense of urgency. And he found making and sustaining teams indispensable.

In the fall of 2020 with the arrival of vaccines on the horizon, JP started thinking through how the county would distribute them. "If we couldn't find toilet paper," he reasoned, "then we won't be able to find vaccinations, either." As he saw it, the usual medical system would not rush in on a great white horse; they were struggling to keep up with what they already were responsible for. His department had not housed vaccines for several years, so he started seeking others who could help. He found our company since we were working in Pierce County already with the flu shot project. JP approached us with a simple request: Please help us figure out the best way for our county to support local access to COVID vaccinations when they arrive. Real, useful humility takes a lot of courage. JP's courageous humility brought him to ask the right questions about how to prepare for the vaccine.

We knew that from a business perspective, this request was no guarantee of a financially sustainable project. Find and organize a few people for a few hours a week to do brainstorming and planning: that is not how you make money. Better to keep hiring staff for projects in larger counties. As a staffing company, our income was based on how many people were working a full day. But we also knew that Lewis County was precisely where the need was greatest. I had been a primary care doctor there and still worked in their hospital. Health measurements such as longevity, healthy behaviors, and access consistently ranked Lewis County near the bottom of the state.[1]

"What do you want me to tell Lewis County?" Patrick asked me one evening while we reviewed payroll hours on Zoom.

"We're already stretched," I said. I looked at the clock—it was 10 PM.

"It doesn't sound too hard to me," Patrick said, ever the optimist. Patrick may underestimate the difficulty of things because of his own capabilities. His fluency in Chinese hides the fact that he only started learning it in college. Most of us do not have his extensive talents or persistence.

"We did ask God and the health departments to tell us what they wanted us to do—remember praying that?" I asked. Patrick did remember, and he recalled the many things we tried when nobody was asking for our help. At least this time around, others were seeking us

[1] Christine Muganda et. al., *County Health Rankings & Roadmaps: 2022 State Report Washington* (University of Wisconsin Population Heath Institute, 2022), https://www.countyhealthrankings.org/sites/default/files/media/document/CHR2022_WA_0.pdf.

out. I continued: "But we can't do it by ourselves. We will have to add a leader for this project. If we can't find one, we should say no. You are right, it shouldn't be that technically challenging—we take what we are learning from Pierce County down the interstate to Lewis County."

Dr. Mary Ellen Biggerstaff was the first person I called. Dr. Biggerstaff is a very capable nurse practitioner I worked with for several years at the rural hospital in Elma, Washington. She had a master's degree in public health, and I knew she would relish the chance to do more in this field. Her personality would be the perfect complement to mine. She can disagree without either getting angry or stirring up others' anger. Her patience would be invaluable in county planning meetings.

Dr. Biggerstaff immediately agreed to help. She was excited to work on COVID issues after so many months of feeling underutilized. With her on board, we were able to say yes to Lewis County. Mary Ellen started going to meetings on Zoom and in person. The county soon added multiple community stakeholders and built a team that represented the county well. Dr. Biggerstaff would report what they talked about, and I would start to criticize: "Why didn't you say this? Why would someone think that?" Then I remembered that she was the public health expert and that we had hired her because she had skills I lacked. Dr. Biggerstaff quickly identified turf issues and politics. The whole program needed to be on the community's terms, not ours. JP and Dr. Biggerstaff both had to keep that principle front and center, or the community would have kicked our team out. At the same time, they had to move forward with urgency—asking for too much input would slow the process down. At times, JP and Dr. Biggerstaff each felt the other was dragging their feet, though both were anxious to get vaccines out quickly and safely.

Patrick and I realized we needed an additional person to help think through logistics issues regarding mass vaccinations. Who does traffic control and how? What if people need to go to the bathroom? What radio station is best to announce an event? I advertised for someone to help with planning for now and maybe work more regularly later. From many capable applicants, I hired Kevin Sublette, a Lewis County resident with loads of experience organizing auctions. Kevin had lost two high school buddies to COVID and was ready to fight that monster. I was impressed with how he immediately saw the potential and the needs at the fairgrounds and how well he got along with the county leaders there when we did a walk-through. Kevin had many insights in the planning stage. But would that translate into pulling off this complex project with its medical components that Kevin had never worked with before?

The Lewis County group explored many options. We noted that the usual system of pharmacies and some doctors' offices giving all the vaccines within a few months was not going to work. Even if every pharmacy gave 50 shots every day, it would take five months to vaccinate the whole county. And if the pharmacists spent all their time giving shots, nobody could get any other medications. Obviously, we would have to supplement the regular system with mass vaccination events. That way we could give up to 4,000 shots per day, and it would not need to be every day. But who would run these events? Where would they happen? How would we get the medical personnel? What about people without transportation? Who would educate and advertise? How could we make sure the elderly in the various institutions had access? What about minority groups? Those without insurance? Inmates at the county jail?

Many local people and groups collaborated in this process. This included the small local health and emergency management departments, Twin City Transit (now Lewis County Transit), Providence, Arbor Health, The Equity Institute, United Way, Valley View's clinics, and others. They all brought energy. Yet we felt the basic plans for vaccinating large numbers were not quite gelling. They were getting close, but would they be ready on time? Dr. Biggerstaff, Patrick, and I did not want to push Lewis County to do what they did not want to do, but it seemed like they needed a nudge. They had asked us for our recommendations. What would we recommend? After considering several large open spaces, we encouraged them to use the Southwest Washington Fairgrounds since it was not in use and was conducive to a drive-through. For staffing, the county planned to rely heavily on volunteers. We supported this but were concerned that volunteers would only be able to give so much, would be less predictable, and would not provide all the medically trained people needed. Without at least some paid staff, we worried that Lewis County would not be able to pull off the mass vaccinations.

"How is the planning?" I asked Dr. Biggerstaff on a Zoom call one day, with her and Patrick as little boxed faces on my computer.

"It's very good," she replied. "Everyone has such good things to say, and people are getting along."

"And the plan? Do we have a working plan to give mass vaccinations?" I asked.

"Well, not exactly. We have a lot of agreement, but the various stakeholders are not quite sure. Some wonder if we really need mass vaccinations, and others are not sure where…"

"What do you mean?" I was starting to raise my voice, but Patrick deftly interrupted.

"Dr. Bunge, I think Dr. Mary Ellen is saying they are working hard on it."

"Government workers can work hard on something for years and achieve nothing," I said without thinking.

"Remember that's why you don't go to those meetings," Patrick reasoned.

"Then what do we do?" I asked, frustrated.

"Why don't we make our own plan and present it?" asked Patrick.

Dr. Biggerstaff agreed. "It can't hurt. I don't think anyone will be offended, though they won't be ready to say yes quite yet. It might move the discussion along."

It seemed like a waste of time to me if it wasn't going to be used, but Patrick and I spent hours hammering out a proposal for the county, outlining what we considered to be the best approach to implement mass vaccinations. We calculated how many staff it would take to completely run a day of mass vaccinations at the fairgrounds without volunteers, but in a way that we could substitute volunteers if they were available. We itemized needed equipment and supplies, how many bathrooms we would need, and other expenses. When we totaled the cost of the proposal, we knew the county would experience sticker shock, but we also knew that failing to realistically plan for mass vaccination made it much less likely to happen. We prayed and sent in the proposal.

The answer was no, we would not be doing this plan. Their answer did not surprise us, and we continued to meet, discuss, and support the team.

Chapter Eleven: The Vaccines Arrive

It is the glory of God to conceal a matter, but the glory of kings is to search out a matter.

– Proverbs 25:2 (NASB)

We cannot control anyone's reactions but our own. Therefore, we shouldn't work to please others or to gain their approval; we must, instead, set our own goals and work to satisfy those. When faced with setbacks or failures, we mustn't blame others; assigning blame keeps us focused on things over which we have no power. Instead, we can respond to misfortune by learning more, working harder, and being more creative.

– Katalin Kariko[1]

O n December 11, 2020, Pfizer received emergency approval for its COVID vaccine, and Moderna's was approved soon after. The New England Journal of Medicine articles on these vaccines[2] showed

---

[1] Katalin Kariko, *Breaking Through: My Life in Science* (Crown, 2023), 50.

[2] For the Pfizer vaccine: Fernando Polack et al., "Safety and Efficacy of the BNT162b2 mRNA Covid-19 Vaccine," *New England Journal of Medicine* 383, no. 27 (2020), https://doi.org/10.1056/NEJMoa2034577.

For the Moderna vaccine: Lindsey Baden et al., "Efficacy and Safety of the mRNA-1273 SARS-CoV2 Vaccine," *New England Journal of Medicine* 384, no. 5 (2020), 403–416, https://doi.org/10.1056/NEJMoa2035389.

dramatic results with a greater than 90% reduction in COVID infection, and especially relevant, the near elimination of clinically dangerous infections. They were more effective than anyone had thought possible. The US took longer than some countries to make a vaccine available, but once we did, we had solid evidence that these vaccines worked, without dangerous side effects in the vast majority of patients. Heavy US government investment fueled the development of the vaccines as well as their manufacturing and distribution. This included coordination between multiple federal departments, including the Department of Defense, and numerous private corporations. This reflected the complexity and interconnectedness of modern economies and national and international supply chains.[1]

The COVID vaccines were a breakthrough. Previously, vaccines were mostly made from a weaker virus or a weakened form of the same virus. The first published evidence of vaccination was a description in 1798 by Jenner, who scraped material from cowpox lesions, made small cuts in the skin of the uninfected, and rubbed that material into the cuts to prevent smallpox.[2] We now know that the milder cowpox virus is similar genetically to smallpox and produces an effective immunity against it. It was a great breakthrough, especially as smallpox was a leading cause of death, killing 10–20% of those infected, and leaving many others permanently scarred and sometimes blind.

Most vaccines currently used are still made from other viruses, either killed or weakened, and sometimes genetically altered to carry just enough of the target disease's DNA or RNA that the body can make viral proteins and then mount an immune response to them. Thanks to vaccines, many diseases that used to ravage children are mostly a thing of the past, including measles, German measles, polio, and mumps. With more effective and safer vaccines than Jenner's, and a targeted

---

[1] Chad Brown and Thomas Bollyky, "How COVID-19 vaccine supply chains emerged in the midst of a pandemic," *The World Economy* 45, no. 2 (2022), 468–522, https://doi.org/10.1111/twec.13183.
[2] Stefan Riedel, "Edward Jenner and the History of Smallpox and Vaccination," *Baylor University Medical Center Proceedings* 18, no. 1 (2005), 21–25, https://doi.org/10.1080/08998280.2005.11928028.

international vaccine effort, smallpox was eliminated from the earth—the last human case was recorded in 1977.

Similar technology was used to develop COVID vaccines in China, Russia, and for the Janssen vaccine in the US: altering a virus to contain a few sections of RNA from COVID-19. Enough for the body to make some COVID proteins and get an immune response, but not the full RNA that could produce more virus. The Moderna and Pfizer vaccines do not use viruses at all. They use an entirely new technology to get portions of RNA into the cell. The story started in Hungary, where a hard-working young biologist, Katalin Kariko, became fascinated with the messenger molecule of the cell: mRNA.[1]

Dr. Kariko moved to Pennsylvania in 1985 looking for work after her research lab in Hungary ran low on money. She spent most of the next 30-plus years working on messenger RNA, looking for ways to stimulate the body's cells to fight off disease. For most of that time, her research was considered fringe: she had many failures in the lab, had trouble getting grant money, and had to jump from lab to lab, never gaining seniority. But she maintained the conviction that she was on to a useful tool for medical treatments, as she knew from prior animal studies that if you could get RNA into the cell, the cell would produce that RNA's protein.

Dr. Kariko later joined Dr. Drew Weissman, who saw potential in her RNA research. Finally, two cutting-edge biotech firms added further funding: Moderna in the US, and BioNTech in Germany (later partnered with Pfizer). Nanotechnology was used to add micro-sized lipid spheres to hold the RNA so it could get into the cells. Because the lipid spheres are of the same material that lines the cells and because the particles are so small, they attach to the cells and let the RNA in. The human cell machinery then sees that messenger RNA and makes COVID proteins out of it. It only has bits of that RNA: it cannot make a whole virus, and the person does not get infected. The body's DNA is not altered. Those proteins cause the person's immune system to respond and develop a

---

[1] Material summarized from her book and: Gina Kolata, "Long Overlooked, Kati Kariko Helped Shield the World From the Coronavirus," *New York Times*, April 8, 2021, https://www.nytimes.com/2021/04/08/health/coronavirus-mrna-kariko.html.

resistance to COVID. Doctors Kariko and Weissman received the Nobel Prize in 2023 for their groundbreaking work.

Pierce County received its first shipment of Moderna COVID vaccines in the second half of December 2020. They did small events with drive-through vaccinations, but only for certain high-risk groups and medical people. They didn't have enough vaccines to do large drive-through events yet, but they were preparing for the large shipments to come, and our nurses were to help. Each state had the final decision on how to prioritize who would get the vaccines first, usually following CDC guidance. So many people were anxious to get their shot, and it was difficult to wait.

Patrick texted me one day and asked for a Zoom meeting. It was still novel to have our own company Zoom account, work at home, and have instant connections. How quickly the novelty would be replaced by a longing for the presence of real people, but it worked for what we needed.

"Dr. Bunge," Patrick began, always slow to bring out the tough part. He had started calling me Dr. Bunge instead of Paul, as he explained it, to encourage the employees to respect my position and build an atmosphere of trust around medical decisions—mine and others. I can't say I don't appreciate the respect, though typically I am not much bothered by what people call me. Patrick continued: "Ellen from Pierce County says there isn't nearly enough space or people to manage all the vaccines they are going to need." Patrick let that sink in for a while. Did he know what he was asking? I am still never quite sure. But he was doing exactly what I had tasked him with: go find out what is needed and let's see if we can do it.

"What are you saying? Do you want me to load up my kitchen fridge with vaccines?" I asked once my thoughts were sorted after this left-field request. "What about the hospitals? What about the private pharmacies? And is Ellen crazy?"

"Ellen says they looked into the hospitals and pharmacies. They don't have the capacity at Emergency Management, and the County Health Department's fridges and personnel just won't be enough." Patrick had already reviewed with me some of the drama between county departments. Was this request the result of politics or an actual need? Much later, I would see for myself their capabilities—they were correct to ask for help, but I had no idea at the time. We would have to trust them. I could have said no. I could have tried to ask Jennifer to support hiring a slew of pharmacists and renting somewhere. She would have said no: we did not have the money to hire that kind of extensive crew, and nobody had vaccine fridges anyway. I didn't know what to say, so I avoided a direct answer.

"When do they want us to start, and what are the steps?" I asked. *That's not a commitment, is it? Isn't it just a question?* I thought.

Patrick was silent. Why say what is obvious when it is painful? Of course, it would need to be right away. And of course, neither one of us had any clue about vaccine storage rules, shipping, and the rest. "I'll stop by Home Depot on the way home," he said. "And my mom has a freezer in her basement she isn't using." Patrick is creative, focused, and hard working. I appreciated him very much. At the same time, I knew this was a big unknown and it would be complicated. I already had a patient list with a whole county on it, and I was trying to get used to this public health role. Would I need to add vaccine storage to my duties as well?

Jennifer was in the home office listening in on our conversation. I am sure she rolled her eyes at me seriously considering taking on vaccine storage by myself. But she didn't try to pull me back. She did not see the COVID patients in the hospital, she did not follow the medical updates, and she was bored by my monologues on COVID. But she was behind this project. She knew the country needed vaccines, and she knew the work that we were doing was important, with the caveat that she didn't want money to be wasted.

Jennifer came behind my desk to give me a side hug as I sat in my chair. At the same time, both of Patrick's girls came into view on the screen in their pajamas. They knew us well from our families spending time together both in China and the US. Jennifer started talking to the kids in Chinese, and they easily responded. For Jennifer, it was still a wonder to see a blond kid fluent in Mandarin. Our business, the lives of millions, the pandemic, isolation, and the weight of the dollar, all went on pause as weightless, magical words of children floated between screens. God bless that beautiful, elvish family.

I read everything I could about vaccine storage and went through the CDC's and the state's online training. Patrick and I put together the jumble of state paperwork to become a certified vaccine storage site. I connected with St. Peter Hospital's young, intelligent head pharmacist, Dr. Danny Venhouwer, as well as the head vaccine nurse at Northwest Pediatrics, since pediatric nurses are often the local vaccine authorities with the most experience.

We set up deep freezers and simple refrigerators from Home Depot and started monitoring temperatures inside. We discovered that a chest freezer keeps a steady temperature easily, even a nonmedical one. Refrigerators are a different story. In a residential refrigerator, the top shelf is warmer and the bottom colder. When the door opens, the whole thing heats up quickly. Or the area near the freezer is too cold, which is why mixed fridge-freezer units are not allowed in the program. A medical-grade refrigerator has two basic features: a tight temperature regulation system, and powerful fans that circulate the air when the door is closed.

We didn't bother ordering a medical-grade freezer, as a regular chest-type deep freezer worked just fine. The nonmedical refrigerators we took back to Home Depot—I would not accept that quality. While we were doing our testing, we did look at medical-grade fridges and freezers, finding out quickly how disrupted the supply chains were due to the pandemic and friction with China. We could order them, but they might not arrive for months to years. They were all made in China, even when they carried an American label. Every county wanted one for the same reason we did. We also had to have special thermometers to reliably record temperatures 24 hours a day. Pierce County lent us a couple of those, and we got busy ordering more.

We ordered a small medical-grade fridge, which didn't come for months. We were able to find some portable medical plug-in coolers that are used to transport donated organs, blood, and the like. We bought four of these and kept our eyes out for more.

I then found time to do two weeks of testing temperatures in the coolers before I accepted any vaccines. These small coolers did not have fans, so I had to find another way to maintain the proper temperatures. Since water holds a more consistent temperature than air, I experimented with water bottles in various configurations inside the coolers. With that and some babysitting, they kept a constant temperature. Especially when we had some frozen vaccines that needed to be thawed to fridge temperature, I spent many hours in the vaccine room, checking temperatures every hour and listening for the temperature alarms. I felt like I was taking care of a new baby.

Strangely, with all the rules and regulations regarding vaccines and the vaccine programs in Washington State, there was no requirement to have a backup power source. We were required to have a place to take our vaccines if our cooling system failed, so we made an agreement with the local Providence hospital. But what if everyone's fridge was full and thousands of doses were at risk? I didn't want to be the guy on the news who lost a bunch of vaccines to a power outage. But I needed something quick—I couldn't wait for the installation of a big, expensive backup system. Plus, we needed something easy to transport when we got more office space.

The solution I found was large camping batteries. I picked up a Yeti 500X lithium battery to serve as backup power to my small fridges. We could use that at the vaccine site as well. The freezer plugged into a larger 1500X battery which in turn plugged into the wall. Instant backup.[1] I also bought some simple plug-in alarms for the vaccine room. If the power went out, everyone within a block would know.

By the time I was ready to store vaccines, we were already supplying nurses to the COVID vaccine events that Pierce County was able to do. Lewis County was making progress, but no large events there yet. What about the lives of the rural folks?

---

[1] We continued to improve our backup system over time. The next step was to get a power switch that would automatically change the power source from the wall to the battery when the power went out. After much searching, we found one designed for boats: the Xantrex PROwatt SW, model: PROWATT SW AUTO TRANSFER SWITCH. The Xantrex company helpfully confirmed the safety of the setup I made with the Yeti battery backup.

Chapter Twelve:
Right Person, Right Gear, Right Job

Then Saul dressed David in his own tunic. He put a coat of armor on him and a bronze helmet on his head. David fastened on his sword over the tunic and tried walking around, because he was not used to them. "I cannot go in these," he said to Saul, "because I am not used to them." So he took them off. Then he took his staff in his hand, chose five smooth stones from the stream, put them in the pouch of his shepherd's bag and, with his sling in his hand, approached the Philistine.
> *– I Samuel 17:38–40 (NIV)*
> *(David preparing to meet Goliath)*

The power of human nature is that, unlike other forces of nature, it is not uniform. Instead, its power lies in its idiosyncrasy, in the fact that each human's nature is different.
> *– Marcus Buckingham & Curt Coffman[1]*

A ll our nurses knew how to give shots, and they were doing just that in Pierce County. But now we would be responsible for coordinating vaccine storage and getting vaccines to the nurses. This

---

[1] Marcus Buckingham and Curt Coffman, *First, Break All the Rules: What the World's Greatest Managers Do Differently* (Simon & Schuster, 1999), 242.

on-site management was not as complicated as the overall program of storing the vaccines, but it still required skill that not everyone possessed. We could pull nurses from giving shots to manage this, but nurses were hard to come by. How could we find the right people for this job? Or could we train them ourselves?

Kylie Bretzel had worked on our school testing project, doing paperwork to check people in. It was a job for which, with her master of public health, she was overqualified. Kylie had grown up in Tacoma. Her father had come from Hawaii. Major influences in her life included church, her perfectionist mother, and her loving and supportive Hawaiian grandmother. She went to Hawaii for college and stayed to work in public health. Recently back in Tacoma, she was unemployed largely due to COVID. She felt useless, missed the close-knit Hawaii culture, and felt guilty taking unemployment payments.

I decided to call her: "Kylie, this is Dr. Bunge from Bird's Eye Medical, where you helped with COVID testing."

"Oh, Dr. Bunge, yes, of course," said Kylie brightly. "I appreciated the chance to work at the schools!"

"I wonder if you would be interested in more work." I explained that we weren't sure if it would all work, that she would have to be licensed through the state system, that she would have to take online training and do other reading, and then there would be more in-person orientation. I could hardly get the description out, she was so ready to get back to work.

To get her up to speed, we sent Kylie to spend time with Tacoma's public health nurses. She and I also worked vaccine clinics together as the larger shipments started arriving for Pierce County. She was a quick study. As vaccine manager, she was conscientious and strong enough to hold her own when nurses came in to get new vials: "Sorry, you have to come back with your paperwork and the empty vial first," she would say. She was not being rude. We had to meticulously track vials, doses, and paperwork. Not many people could sit all day in the RV (or the cold tent, or the portable building, depending on where we kept the vaccines at that particular site), monitor everything going on, redirect a nurse or two, and work with the site manager, usually a salty ambulance driver.

The state approved our site to receive and store vaccines. Our first batch was a thousand doses transferred from the Tacoma-Pierce County Health Department. Kylie and I picked them up with our portable coolers.

The state had special rules for "remote" vaccination clinics, written for the rare occasion when someone wasn't giving vaccines in the office or pharmacy. We had to follow these extra rules as every event for us was "remote," which meant many extra temperature checks and more paperwork.

I was terrified of messing up. What if our coolers failed and the vaccines were ruined? What if I didn't follow the rules closely enough and the state declared our site unfit? In my nervousness, the first few times we transported vaccines, I had Kylie follow me in her car with a second cooler just in case I had a car accident.

Early on, one of the vials lodged deep in the cooler between water bottles and our count was off, causing no little stir with the county. But I found it a few days later, still at the proper temperature, and we could still use it. Thankfully, that was our worst mistake. We heard reports of whole batches of vaccines being lost due to power outages. One hospital in Seattle caught the frowning attention of the governor's office when it invited certain donors to get their vaccines early, ahead of the people at highest risk who should have received them.[1] When the Department of Health later sent out a team to survey COVID storage across the state, they said ours was a model for others. By that time, we had several employees helping with vaccine storage and monitoring, but in the beginning, it was just me and my raw nerves.

One night I dreamed that all the vaccines I was storing started to hatch like eggs. I watched in horror as thousands of vaccine vials shook violently and broke open. Out of each vial popped a small version of me: thin, bespectacled, with a red cap and striped shirt like Waldo from the "Where's Waldo?" books. They ran around my house and then out

---

[1] Evan Bush, Mike Reicher, and Sydney Brownstone, "Overlake medical center donors got special access to COVID-19 vaccine; Inslee rebukes hospital system," *The Seattle Times*, January 6, 2021, https://www.seattletimes.com/seattle-news/times-watchdog/special-access-to-covid-19-vaccine-for-overlake-medical-center-donors-draws-inslee-rebuke/

the door. I desperately ran after them, calling out, "Where are you going? Don't leave! We need you!" That was when I realized I could use some breathing room and it was not healthy for me to be the only one responsible for thousands of COVID doses 24 hours a day, 7 days a week with no end in sight, besides my other jobs. But I was stuck until we got a bigger office and a medical-grade refrigerator.

The Pierce County project was going well. We provided nursing staff and support staff. We took turns providing vaccines to events, alternating with the county health department and later with another company.

As we were supplying vaccines, we were expected to enter patient data into the state's tracking system, which we had not anticipated. These systems, required by the federal government, were put in place primarily to allow patients and providers to access vaccine records to help keep people (especially kids) up to date on their vaccines. The programs predate most current electronic medical records and are antiquated and difficult to use. The Washington State Immunization Information System (WAIIS—we called it "waze") was also used for ordering and tracking vaccines. After each event, we wound up with between 1,000 and 4,000 papers that people had filled out, and we had to enter them individually into the WAIIS system. A state regulation required us to do this within 24 hours of the shot (or 72 hours in "extenuating circumstances"). We started offering our employees work on "data days" after the vaccine events. Our first data days were quite a challenge. When it was available, we set up at the Pierce County Department of Emergency Management (DEM) command room. Some days I had people lined up in my living room at portable tables. Roberta did the same at her house.

"I am done with my stack of papers," I said to my daughter, Erika, one night. Erika was helping me with data entry since she was home, after quitting her scribe job in Seattle. She mostly did it out of mercy to me, seeing how overstretched and stressed I was. More staff had been working in our living room earlier that day, but they hadn't finished by late afternoon, so Erika and I were trying to finish up before it got too late at night.

"I doubt that you are really done," she said in response.

"What do you mean?" I investigated our lockbox to see if I had overlooked some papers.

"You probably missed filling out some of the required blocks," Erika said, not looking up from her own data entry. She had only given me one quarter of the stack since she was so much faster than I was. Was it a generational thing?

Of course she was right and I had to go back in and add to every one of my files. Erika finished long before I did, helped complete my meager stack, and ran the double checks on our data. How I longed to be free from data entry!

We soon had employees entering data nearly every day. We made it work. Although there were plenty of people like me who hated doing it, were slow, and longed for the day when it would be over, I noticed a curious thing: some people loved it. They not only entered the data all day long, but they also together came up with creative ways to double-check and triple-check, improving efficiency and accuracy.

"Maybe we are approaching this the wrong way," I told Patrick one day. "Instead of being annoyed at data entry, maybe this is an area of need that we could step into, as long as we have motivated people who can be accurate."

Carlin Devorss and Brian Handy were friends of Roberta's son in high school. She told them we had posted for people to help with data entry, and Carlin thought it might be a good spring break job, so the two boys found themselves working in Roberta's living room instead of only coming over to visit. They signed up together to support each other, as they both struggled with social anxiety.

One day they were entering data in Tacoma, and Patrick said: "You two are doing a great job! You are exactly the kind of workers we need."

"I have a strong resistance to tedium and boredom," said Carlin.

"So you don't want to do the data work?" asked Patrick, confused.

"Actually," said Carlin, "I know it may bore most people, but I love this work. I play nerdy computer games with plenty of numbers, and doing this is not much different. It keeps my attention. Other things I would rather just pawn off on other people."

Patrick smiled at Carlin's deadpan humor, but he wasn't sure where the line was between his joking and reality.

We created data teams and kept a list of folks who were motivated and were consistently accurate, including Brian and Carlin. Kylie got much of our overall WAIIS system started, and Madi Hubble later took over using WAIIS to order and track vaccines. We implemented our own double-check tracking system for vaccines as we started sending them to more and more places. When we looked for an office, we knew we needed a large room to line up computers for data entry and space for a row of filing cabinets.

The need for a better data entry software was painfully obvious to everyone involved. "I heard the Pierce County people debating whether they should ask Solv to help them with their vaccine data," Patrick told me one day, "or whether they should wait for the state's plan, which sounds like using PrepMod—a program developed by a nonprofit in Massachusetts."

"Solv is great," I said. "King County is using it at their COVID testing sites, and it is so easy to use as a patient." When I needed a COVID test a few months before, I signed up on Solv's interface online and went to a drive-through run by firemen in King County. I was very impressed. "It was easy to sign myself up, put in my insurance information, and get through the line at the drive-through." I explained to Patrick that medical practices and hospitals never let you register yourself into their system, thinking you would mess it up. Solv had apparently ignored that worry and seemed to be doing okay.

"Makes sense," said Patrick. "What is going to operate better, a program that is already functional and easy to use, or something made by an unknown nonprofit on the East Coast?"

A few days later, Erika and Kylie came into my office to discuss software for the Lewis County project. As my daughter, Erika ignored some of the general respect a boss gets, like knocking or saying hello. "PrepMod is a good program, and it's going to work," she said.

"Dr. Bunge," added Kylie more politely. "We were just on a Zoom training, and it looks to me like here is a program that the county doesn't need to pay for, that has the capability to schedule patients, store the needed data, and interact with the state's required system. I think we should use it for Lewis County." I quickly put Dr. Biggerstaff on speaker phone since she was the project lead for Lewis County.

"I know you want to go with Solv, Dr. Bunge," said Dr. Biggerstaff, "and you and I have been through electronic medical nightmares together." We both laughed, recalling the implementation of a program at the hospital in Elma, which soon had to be replaced because the outpatient module was missing key functions.

"If it doesn't work, we will have to use paper as backup," I said. They had not convinced me, but I was willing to let them decide.

"We know," said Kylie. "We will be ready with paper if we need it."

But would we even use this program at all? We were going strong in Pierce County but had not had even one mass vaccination in Lewis County. What was the holdup?

Chapter Thirteen: Stirring the Pot

I know your deeds, your hard work, and your perseverance.
— Revelation 2:2a (NIV)

We are continually faced with a series of great opportunities brilliantly disguised as insoluble problems.
— John Gardner[1]

L ewis County was still behind. It wasn't for lack of planning: by now, the various groups had worked out a pathway forward, which closely resembled our plan that had initially been rejected. Mass vaccination would be at the Southwest Washington Fairgrounds location. We would use volunteers for as much of the work as possible, and Bird's Eye Medical would provide leaders as well as medical personnel as needed when there were not enough volunteers. We had the workers lined up. We had our paperwork, computers, and rain gear. Our internet sign-up system was up and running. The Transit Department was ready with transportation and had set up a call center to answer questions and help schedule those who were unable to sign up online. We were ready. But there were no vaccines. The state received only so many per week, and they had not allocated any to Lewis County mass vaccination.

---

[1] Emily DiNuzzo, "51 Life-Changing Quotes You Won't Forget," Reader's Digest Web Page, Accessed Nov 26, 2024, https://www.rd.com/list/life-changing-quotes/.

Meanwhile, our work in Pierce County was going full steam ahead. Thankfully, we were able to use the Moderna vaccine. It was much easier to work with than Pfizer's, which had to be stored at -80 degrees Celsius and which, once thawed to refrigerator temperature, had to be used within a week.[1]

Lewis County's public health director, JP Anderson, was frustrated and decided to stir the pot. During his regular public health announcement, he mentioned that Lewis County was not getting attention in the vaccine rollout. He talked to both State Representative Peter Abbarno and State Senator John Braun. The local paper picked these moves up and harshly criticized the state for putting the lives of rural folks last.[2] Though the allocation had already been determined for that week, we got a call from JP's office: We are getting several thousand doses, and you need to give them out. But it wasn't all good news: we were getting Pfizer, not Moderna.

If anyone needed those shots, it was the people of Lewis County. Our project leaders got right to work, shifting gears for Pfizer shots. Kylie was ready to be the site coordinator, making the long trek to Lewis County. But working with Pfizer for the first time brought new challenges. How would we store it? We didn't have a "super-freezer" that cooled to -80 degrees, and keeping it on dry ice as some were doing seemed even more difficult and risky.

Rachel Loukas is a Doctor of Pharmacy we had hired to help give vaccines in Pierce County. I gave her a frantic call. "We are getting Pfizer shots. None of us has any experience with them, and we are not prepared!"

"Oh, they're not so bad," said Rachel, who never came unglued. "I have been giving Pfizer shots at my part-time job at CVS Pharmacy. I can help."

---

[1] This requirement to use the Pfizer within a week was later relaxed after more evaluations of the vaccine's stability.

[2] Claudia Yaw, "'I Think Our Concerns Were Heard': Lewis County Allocated 2000 Vaccine Doses," *The Chronicle*, February 24, 2021, https://www.chronline.com/stories/i-think-that-our-concerns-were-heard-lewis-county-allocated-2000-vaccine-doses,259379.

She briskly churned out training plans and Standard Operating Procedures (SOPs) needed to manage the Pfizer shots. I wrote standing orders to authorize our nurses to administer the vaccine. We trained nurses.

Roberta and the rest of us kept recruiting and hiring. The delay in finalizing the plan contributed to the urgency to get moving once the vaccines were available. I stopped by Providence Centralia Hospital and begged. The county sent out faxes to all the providers' offices: please come and volunteer! Roberta found the staffing role a big challenge and has a new respect for the administrative side of medicine.

I found out that Providence St. Peter Hospital had the only -80 degree freezer within multiple counties.[1] The first couple of times I called, the answer was no, we could not use any of that valuable space. I called up Dr. Kevin Caserta, medical director for St. Peter and Centralia, and explained the need. He made some calls. St. Peter's head pharmacist, Danny Venhouwer, called me shortly afterwards. "We should have room in our -80 freezer."

"Great," I replied. "How will we access the vials once they are stored there?"

"Just tell us the day before how many vaccines you will need. We'll thaw them to fridge temperature and have them ready to go in the morning."

"Awesome," I said, relieved. "Kylie will drive down from Tacoma to pick them up and bring them to the fairgrounds in Centralia with a portable cooler." As I spoke, I reflected on how we had been able to shift Kylie so quickly from Pierce to Lewis County. An intriguing Vietnamese American named Long Nguyen was the reason.

Long had applied for the Bird's Eye Medical logistics position in Lewis County. We hired Kevin instead, but I kept Long's file, anticipating that such a capable person would surely be useful somewhere. Could this engineer work on-site with vaccines in Pierce County so we could move Kylie down to Lewis?

---

[1] We heard one of the schools in Lewis County may have had a very low-temperature freezer for their science program, but that seemed impractical and did not solve the issue of who would monitor and access it.

When I talked to Long, he was interested but had many questions. Was this a good sign, that as a detailed person, he would pay close attention to the vaccines and their rules? Or would an obsession with details grind things to a halt? Could he work with nurses and the Tacoma EMS staff? We decided to give him a chance.

Kylie and I trained Long at Pierce County events. He picked things up quickly and did not mind working in the inhospitable places where the vaccines were stored, depending on where the event was that day. Long kept meticulous control of the vaccine vials, yet at the same time he would boisterously talk it up with the ambulance drivers through his thick accent, always with a smile.

Long Nguyen was no stranger to challenges. Things in Vietnam were bad and not getting better in 1986. His parents had heard there was a chance for a better life, but they had not heard from Long's older brother since they put him on a boat out of the country two years before. Long remembers it as a kind of game when his family took him and his two sisters down to the dock. He was with his siblings—what could go wrong? He was nine years old.

The boat captain took only gold for payment since Vietnamese money had become almost worthless. The overloaded craft surged into the open ocean, where six days later a larger boat found them and towed them to Indonesia. His brother's boat had not been so fortunate.

Long woke up from his "vacation" with a jolt when he and his sisters landed at their first foster home in the US. There, the alcoholic father soon took to beating the children. That's when he realized that there was no going back to his parents. Many nights, at least one of the three cried themselves to sleep.

Catholic Social Services transferred the children to a home in Seattle after 14 months. Less than a year later, those foster parents had an accident, and the children were back in Tacoma. The three were in foster home number four when the older sister turned 18, became guardian for the other two, and was able to get them an apartment. Long worked part-time jobs through high school and college. Even during the first few years of his engineering job, he kept up his after-hours work as a lab tech. He worked for 20 years as an engineer at Genie, renowned Seattle-area maker of scissor lifts. He and his sisters sponsored other family members from Vietnam until the whole brood made it over. He somehow made time to help raise nephews and nieces in various cities around the state.

"I am happy to be doing this work," Long told me one day. "I missed the lab job I used to have."

"Were you thinking about medical school?" I asked.

"Of course," said Long. "But I knew that I couldn't delay making money. We all needed to work as soon as possible to get our family over from Vietnam."

"What was the hardest job you ever did, Long?" I asked.

"Oh, Dr. Bunge," he said. He said that phrase a lot, it seemed: Oh, Dr. Bunge. "Nothing compares to berry picking."

"Berry picking?" I asked, surprised.

"For sure! We had one foster grandmother who took us berry picking in Puyallup when I was still a kid. Berry after berry after berry. All three of us. It seemed endless. Compared to that, everything else has been much easier."

None of us had any worry about Long's work ethic. He allowed many on the team to shift their focus to Lewis County when they were finally assigned vaccines.

I was surprised when Dr. Danny's number from St. Peter's came up on my cell phone. He had never called me unprompted before. "Your vials are safely in our freezer," he said cheerfully. It seemed we were ready for our first Lewis County event. Had we missed something? Were we biting off more than we could chew? I couldn't possibly remember all the details required—were those assigned going to get their individual parts of this complex dance correct? Would vaccine fears clog up the project in this conservative county? Lives were depending on these details that I couldn't completely control, which lost me even more sleep.

"God," I prayed, "Go with us to the fairgrounds, as you went with Moses and the children of Israel into the promised land so long ago. Have mercy on me, the workers, the volunteers, and the people of Lewis County. Deliver us from this plague!"

Chapter Fourteen: Out of the Gate

And let us not grow weary in well-doing, for in due season we shall reap, if we do not lose heart.
                                        – Galatians 6:9 (RSV)

The pessimists are usually right, but it's the optimists who change the world.
                                        – Simon Sinek[1]

The first day of our mass vaccination in Lewis County finally arrived. I made sure I was off from my hospice job that day, but I still couldn't be there when it started. I rushed out of my house around 9 AM. The day smelled like drizzle, but in my nervous excitement, I left my rain jacket in the closet. Half an hour later I pulled into the gravel parking lot of the Southwest Washington Fairgrounds as the rain started that would come and go all day. As I trekked through the fairgrounds, my shoes slowly absorbed the moisture through to my toes.

I marveled at what I saw happening, what I had hoped for since COVID first arrived in the county. A beehive of activity around each node on the line of cars, working in unison.

Thanks to Kevin Sublette's crew, who had been there since

---

[1] Simon Sinek, *Start with Why: How Great Leaders Inspire Everyone to Take Action* (Portfolio/Penguin, 2009), 140. Sinek notes that he is paraphrasing a quote from Thomas Friedman.

predawn, traffic cones and flashing road signs guided the traffic off the main road. Rather than being backed up there like other sites, the cars were funneled into lanes on the fairgrounds themselves. I waved to the registration crew as I passed by, not wanting to distract them too much. This was the first stop for the cars—a quick name and data verification of who was there, since they had mostly entered this online or by phone already.

"This vaccine has been given emergency approval…" I could hear one of the nurses at the counseling tent say as I moved down the line. The canopy tent had no sides and obviously wasn't keeping the crew very dry in even the light rain. But that didn't slow down this team. They were motivated and focused. This was a very important station. It required knowledgeable and educated staff as they fielded many questions. This is where the person would make their final decision on whether to take the vaccine, and plenty of people had questions and fears. I could hear the quality job they were doing as I passed. They explained the vaccine and the process and answered questions.

As I continued my walk, I caught up to Kevin and Kylie as they themselves were checking the stations, busy in chatter: "Next time we should make sure the assignment for each person is printed beside their name at the beginning of the day," Kylie decided out loud.

"The only problem with that is if we have to change roles at the last minute," said Kevin. "But if you make the announcement that morning, that also works."

"Should we keep the paper sign-in sheets for the workers like they do at Pierce County?"

"Don't have to, I think. Once we enter the names and hours into the computer spreadsheet, that should be good. Everyone has a manager to verify their time also. We are not the county, don't need to be such sticklers."

"Did you see that little grandma with her feet dangling in that giant pickup? She was so cute!" said Kylie.

Kevin saw me following them. "Oh hey, Dr. Bunge, when did you get here?"

"Just now," I answered as I shuffled up to them. "How's it going?"

Kevin and Kylie both talked at once and then laughed. That seemed a good sign. Would that laughing continue as the days became weeks and months? Much later, each would talk about the challenge—no, the impossibility—of working with the other. They would find a way through these "impossibilities" again and again. But for now, it was sheer excitement as they saw all the pieces that had come together.

"Hey, Dr. Bunge, could you check on table three?" asked Kylie. "They had some questions I couldn't answer. I was hoping you would be here to clarify for them."

"Oh, and Dr. Bunge," added Kevin, "We need three more walkie-talkies at least."

"Get them if you need them, Kevin," I said. It took a lot of gear to make this work, and it would take more. On the colder days, the nurses had poor Kevin running for propane tanks for portable heaters and chemical hand warmers that never quite got their hands warm enough. "And I'll stop by table three."

Kevin and Kylie resumed their conversation as they walked one way and I went the other: "Kylie, I think we should double-check the Spanish handouts with one more Spanish speaker. Some people gave a funny face…"

But then they were past where I could hear them. Was that knot in my chest finally relaxing after all these months? Were we getting somewhere with COVID? Could we get that daily death count down? My questions moved back to silent prayers as I headed for the vaccine tables. God, please protect these people: workers, volunteers, patients. And thank you that I could be a part of this work.

I met the line of cars again as it turned into the main vaccination area, which we had set up in the cattle barn, a large, covered area without walls. In the winter months, it's rented out for RV and boat storage, but there was still enough room to funnel two lanes of traffic through the middle, with RVs blocking most of the wind. Tables were set up on the sides for each lane.

Each table had at least three staff members—two vaccinators and one scribe who double-checked names, recorded which arm the shot was given in, and reminded people when to get their next shot.

The cars came in three or four at a time, one for each table. Sometimes the line would pause as five or six people in one car all needed shots, while the other cars only had one or two people. The nurses adapted, people were patient with each other, and the whole thing went surprisingly smoothly. After the vaccines were given, cars drove to the main parking area to wait for 15 minutes near the ambulance that was waiting in case of any significant reactions. If someone needed help, they flashed their lights. The ambulance crew walked around checking on people as well. After observation time was over, they were on their way.

I noticed from her name tag that the RN at table three was another Jennifer. "Hello, Jennifer Abelson," I said. "I'm Dr. Bunge."

"Dr. Bunge," Jennifer said loudly as she read my name tag. "Hey, you're our boss!" I guessed she was not known for subtlety. Later, we would think of Jennifer A. first when we had assignments that needed someone with grit who was afraid of nothing. She continued: "I have a question."

"What you got?" I asked.

Jennifer had noticed that you could end up with different brands of needles depending on which supply box you had, and some of them took some getting used to. All had a safety device connected. Most were a plastic piece you pushed from the side to cover the needle after injection. A few of these were very sticky and did not work well (though the injection itself was fine). Jennifer had some of these stubborn ones.[1]

"If you can't easily use the safety device, just put it into the sharps container without engaging it," I decided. We had plenty of sharps containers, and once the needle was inside, there was no risk to the staff or patients.

Overall, the flow was going well. The nurses were motivated. Everyone seemed quite proud to be part of this project. People coming

---

[1] We could not predict which needle safety device would be on which needles from a particular supply box from the CDC. Some were auto-retracting needle-syringe combinations, known by the popular brand name VanishPoint, and a few nurses needed instruction on their use. We found videos and would get extra supplies later when the supply chains caught up so that we could practice with them and substitute our own when needles with poor-quality safety mechanisms showed up. We followed the CDC's instructions to give feedback when we had this type of issue.

for shots often recognized their friends from the community as volunteers or workers, which reassured them.

I completed going around to all the vaccination tables to introduce myself and answer any questions, then crossed the line of cars one more time to get through to the 4-H hall, which served as a temporary office. It was chilly, but dry. We had a secure storage room for supplies, a smaller room for data entry, a small kitchen where we set up our vaccine pharmacy every day, and a large area where staff gathered for the morning orientation and where snacks and lunch were available. When a table ran low on vaccines, someone took their stack of papers to the kitchen and traded them for a new vial and more supplies. The data team then entered the paperwork. A large photocopier/printer was busy printing the handouts we had developed with the county.

"Hello, Rachel," I called over the kitchen counter to our pharmacist, Dr. Rachel Loukas.

"Hello, Dr. Bunge," Dr. Loukas replied from behind her mask. Rachel had an organized system and was always training whoever was with her, though it never seemed like training, only a natural flow of work. I told her about the needle issue, and she said she would check the tables and make sure everyone was using the needles properly and felt comfortable with the different ones.

I was seeing the wisdom of what I had learned in my leadership classes: you must get the right people involved, and then let them make it happen.[1] If I had been less busy, I probably would have micromanaged, and this capable crew might have failed.

My presence may have helped morale that day, and I did some running around to help out. But overall, my anxiety was unfounded. Kylie Bretzel was an attentive, organized leader. Dr. Rachel Loukas had driven from her home 150 miles north, much of the road winding around and over the many fingers of the Puget Sound coastline. A beautiful drive, but not something you would expect someone to undertake several times a week for long days of mass vaccinations in

[1] A key idea in the book: Jim *Collins, Good to Great: Why Some Companies Make the Leap...and Others Don't* (Collins Business, 2001).

the Pacific Northwest winter rains. She was on site that whole day, training, supervising, and giving out the vaccines herself when needed.

That first day with a few hundred vaccines was a success. From there, we were able to debrief, work out kinks, increase efficiency, and increase our capacity to several thousand per day.

Dr. Loukas's commitment to getting the vaccinations out did not stop with Lewis County. She became our ultimate pharmacist resource and go-to person. She wrote and updated procedures. She created an easy-to-read vaccine comparison chart and expanded on it as more became available for different ages and new variants. She trained vaccine managers and scores of vaccinators. Many a Washingtonian received their shots directly from her, as she traveled with vaccine teams all over the state once the mass vaccination sites were no longer needed.

The Lewis County volunteers, organized and vetted by the local United Way, were key to the project's success. Volunteers were more useful and effective than I predicted. But as we had guessed, the mass vaccination would not have happened with volunteers alone. As the volunteer commitment was only for four-hour shifts, our staff had to do training twice a day, but it was doable, as we adapted and expanded Pierce County's daily training system for new people rotating in. Sometimes we had to move a volunteer to a different task, but that was rare.

After picking up a bagel from the snack table, I walked outside to watch the volunteers direct traffic. "My name is John," a well-built, middle-aged man wearing an orange vest over his raincoat introduced himself. I was jealous of the appropriate weather gear. "I keep the cars flowing."

A couple of the corners could be tricky, especially for the larger trucks. The cattle barn was not designed to handle hundreds of vehicles flowing through every day. People like John were keeping bumpers and cement posts from meeting each other.

"Are you keeping warm?" I asked.

"Sure! It helps to walk around. I hate sitting at a desk. I put in my fair share of that over the years."

"Do you have a regular job?" I asked.

"Farming now, which is regularly irregular," he deadpanned. "And

I do have help. And teenagers. So I'm good here during the day."

It was heartwarming to see the community coming together. Humble people working without pay between rows of Ford F150s, doors open so the nurses could reach up into the cab over oversized tires. The United Way coordinators cheerfully greeting their volunteers with motivation and positivity as they came in to work. One or two data-entry people were all we needed for the last step, and then it was all wrapped up by the end of the day.

Not everyone was excited to get their vaccine. There wasn't as much clapping as there was in Pierce County, where fist pumps and cheers were more commonplace after the shot. Often, a driver would say something like, "I don't believe in this vaccine; I am just here to bring my grandma." But there were plenty of people thankful to have this lifesaving shot in their community.

One thing Lewis County could have used more of was trusted messengers, from county officials to police to firefighters to doctors to pastors to schoolteachers to fathers and mothers and grandmothers. Not everyone in local leadership encouraged vaccinations and other COVID public health measures. Lewis County Sheriff Robert Snaza responded to mask mandates with the public comment, "Don't be a sheep."[1] Whatever his purpose in saying this, he missed his chance to encourage people to take the pandemic seriously, and he undermined every other messenger in the county. How many people would be discouraged from taking the vaccine by that type of thinking and messaging in Lewis County? In the whole country? And what was fueling this animosity?

---

[1] Kevin McCarty, "Lewis County Sheriff on video telling crowd, 'don't be a sheep' about wearing face masks," *Kiro 7 News*, June 24, 2020, https://www.kiro7.com/news/local/lewis-county-sheriff-video-telling-crowd-dont-be-sheep-about-wearing-face-masks/YPGYT5XRPFGBNPAODCM4AXV5SY/.

Chapter Fifteen:
The Other Side of the Road

*Do not seek revenge or bear a grudge against anyone among your
people, but love your neighbor as yourself. I am the LORD.*
— Leviticus 19:18 (NIV)

*Every praying Christian, every person who has an encounter with God,
must have a passionate concern for his or her brother or sister, his or
her neighbor. To treat any one of these as if he were less than a child of
God is to deny the validity of one's spiritual experience.*
— Desmond Tutu[1]

"A man was going down from Jerusalem to Jericho." So Jesus
begins a story in answer to questions about who God wants us
to love. Who really is our tribe, our family, our friend? To whom do we
owe basic human decency? Many know the Good Samaritan story. The
man is robbed, beaten, and left for dead. Two religious leaders later
come walking along, one after the other, but each purposely avoids the
man, walking past on the other side of the road. The next person to come
along randomly is a man from Samaria, a non-Jew with an incorrect,
mixed-up theology. But he is the one who is deeply moved. Luke, a

---

[1] Desmond Tutu, *The Words of Desmond Tutu*, comp. Naomi Tutu (New Market Press, 2007), 26.

physician, recorded this story in the Greek language, and used the word esplanchnisthē to describe what the Samaritan felt towards the injured man. In modern medicine's terminology, the "splanchnic system" is the stomach, the intestines, and the related organs, fed by the splanchnic arteries. This man felt a compassion from his very guts. He ran to the suffering man, bandaged him, washed him, and reimbursed his nursing home stay.

Jesus' point was that two educated theologians, paid to be holy and follow the law, looked up to by all the people, were more interested in being on time, remaining unentangled, and getting their dinner than in helping some poor, broken man by the side of the road. If they had pangs of conscience, they were practiced in ignoring them. Perhaps they had perfected their hypocrisy through years of hearing and speaking and writing one thing and doing the opposite. It was the one who had suspect theology, who did not understand the truths of right and wrong and God's plan and what really was God's word, who showed compassion. That person did the right thing, what God wanted, just by following his gut. The Samaritan considered this man his neighbor, though he was unrelated to him, unable to ever pay him back, unlikely to even respect him as a person, much less see him as his neighbor or brother on the road of life. This is a stark warning to all religious people, who can sit in a cushioned pew week after week, or even stand at the pulpit, speaking of love and forgiveness without actually loving or forgiving in the here and now when it requires sacrifice. It should convict all of us who care only for those in our own families, our own tribes, our own sphere of religious agreement.

Jennifer and I have been active in church for decades. We are committed to following the teaching of Scripture, the public preaching of Biblical truths, and spreading the message so that people near and far can hear the good news that God loves them and Jesus died to save them from their sins. We are the religious people, corresponding to the two in Jesus' story. Experts, supposedly, in loving others. In fact, a saying in our church was, "love God, love others," reminding us of Jesus' words from this very parable.

In Jesus' story, the religious people passed by on the other side of the road. During COVID, I felt like I was watching this story repeat over and over, in my patients and across the country. An older man, laying in his hospital bed with COVID, told me he had really tried to minimize contact with others, but he did attend a small group Bible study with his pastor. The pastor who had been to Florida for a large Christian conference, brought COVID back, and shared it.

Most churches at least gave lip service to public health, though some decided to not even do that, resisting public health measures with lawsuits[1] and public stunts.[2] Many churches followed the letter, not the spirit, of public health directives. The whole country bore the poisonous fruit of this hypocritical, nonsense-based approach to public health. This caused faster spread of the disease, worsening confusion, and later religion-themed vaccine fear and apathy. The ultimate result was many unnecessary deaths. We walked purposely on the other side of the road.

In November, Klara, a very good friend living north of Seattle, picked up COVID when her church opened, with much anti-mask sentiment. I gave her medical advice over the phone for several days. She called me one evening, about 10 days into her illness. She still had the trace of a German accent, though she had been in the States since age twelve.

"Dr Paul, I am not breathing that well," she said. She was talking in short sentences and trailing off at the end.

"Did you check your oxygen level?" I asked. I had directed her to order a portable oximeter online and explained how to use it.

"Oh ya, I forgot, let me get it," she replied. Soon she was back on the phone. "It says 72%, is that bad?" she asked, breathing heavily.

"It's time to call the ambulance," I said.

"Oh, that's not necessary," she replied. "I'm sure I will be fine."

[1] Tom Gjelten, "Opposing Church Closures Becomes New Religious Freedom Cause," *NPR*, April 17, 2020, https://www.npr.org/sections/coronavirus-live-updates/2020/04/17/837698597/opposing-forced-church-closures-becomes-new-religious-freedom-cause.
[2] "Pastor holds prayer rally in defiance of coronavirus health guidelines at the California State Capital," *CBS News*, September 8, 2020, https://www.cbsnews.com/news/california-pastor-coronavirus-health-guidelines-prayer-rally/.

"Please, don't argue. It is really time to call the ambulance. Do it for me."

In the end, Klara allowed me to call for her, and pretty soon she was at one of the larger Seattle hospitals. Her sons were out of state, and I called to give them updates. A week later, with Klara worsening, they drove to Seattle.

"Dr. Paul," her son Gerry started on the phone one day. "She has been on the ventilator for six days now. She waves hello to me through the window, so I know she is conscious. But I also know she is miserable, and she looks weaker and weaker. What is going to happen?"

I did my best to give medical information, at the same time trying to be realistic with him. We did not know what would happen. She might pull through, and she might not.

There was another week of deterioration. I was working a seven-day stretch at the Centralia hospital and couldn't answer their calls right away. On my last day, my wife texted me several times. I called both Jennifer and Gerry on my way home that night. It sounded like Klara was not going to make it.

"I know my mom loves Jesus," Gerry said, "I know she is going to a better place. But this is so hard…so very hard."

The next morning, Jennifer was texting with the family again. "Paul, you need to go up there and say hello to that family," she asserted.

"I am pretty worn out," I replied. I had a long list of to-dos that had piled up during my days at the hospital. I also needed to catch up on my sleep. "But if you think that would help them, I will go."

"They are going to take her off the ventilator and let her die," Jennifer said, crying. This woman had been such a blessing to Jennifer and so many others over the years. A guide for those younger than her, always with a listening ear and a comforting word from the Bible. She was a rock in the community, and she had been sorely missed since her husband died and she moved north.

Soon, I was on the highway to Seattle, a slog even with so many people working from home. Jennifer had an important meeting and couldn't come. I met with the family in the parking lot, and we prayed together. I explained what I understood and answered questions. Klara was out of isolation after more than three weeks since the diagnosis, but

I knew I would not be allowed to visit. I was not officially one of her doctors and had never even been to this hospital.

"Where is Gerry?" I asked, noting one son was missing.

"He won't be in until 11," was the reply. People still had businesses to run, jobs to do, even in the shadow of death. I let the family go back into the hospital. Removing the breathing tube (extubation) and turning off the ventilator were to occur after Gerry arrived. My work here was done. I decided to take a nap in the car for a while.

I was startled awake by my cell phone. At first, I could not tell what Jennifer was saying.

"What happened? Did you see Gerry?" she asked. "You need to see him. He was so upset on the phone yesterday."

"OK, I will check with the nurses," I said sleepily. "They may not be at the hospital anymore."

"You need to," Jennifer said.

"OK, I will call them," I said. Surely Klara had passed by now. I had seen enough death and had no desire to see more. But maybe the family was still grieving at the bedside, and I could comfort them on their way out.

After texting and calling Gerry without a response, I went to the hospital front desk to ask if the family was still there. The gentleman manning the desk said a few words on the phone and told me to stand by. Thirty seconds later, a middle-aged nurse in scrubs and a mask whooshed down the hall and looked me straight in the eye: "Are you Dr Bunge?"

I could tell that she was an ICU nurse from her command of the situation. "Yes, I am…" I started, but she had already turned around with a brisk "come with me." I have learned it is wise to listen to the ICU nurse, so I followed her up the steps, through the ICU, and into one of the rooms, though we both knew she was bending rules to let me in.

Klara was still breathing on her own, though weakly, with her two sons on the other side of the bed. I had always admired Klara's strength and wisdom. There she lay unconscious, her body ravaged by the virus and modern medicine's vain attempts to beat it out of her. Gerry asked me how long she had and thanked me for coming. While I put together measly words and they looked at me, I was the only one facing towards the head of the bed. I thought to myself: That may be her last breath—there it goes. I pointed the adult kids back her way, and we stood together on the threshold of heaven. Fare thee well, my friend, it is your time. Though I certainly wish the church had paid you back for your years of service in some way that did not involve this early departure.

The other side of the road.

One group that conservative churches consider outside the realm of true Christians, at least in behavior, is the LGBTQ community. We consider people who are in physical same-sex relationships to be on the wrong path, outside God's best for them. Those who pursue a gender identity different from the one they were physically born with are confused and off track.

Jesus' Good Samaritan story does not make us bristle like it did the conservative Jewish crowd he told it to. They had a low opinion of Samaritans, culturally and theologically. Jesus chose a Samaritan as the hero of his story for its shock value. If Jesus told his story today, we might know it as "The Good Drag Queen," or "Terrorist to the Rescue."

I have spent much of my career clinically training medical students and residents. One of my former trainees was still in the military as an ICU doctor. I called her up to see if she could encourage nurses to contact us for work. She sent her wife, Candace, to help us. We quickly hired this experienced nurse and put her to work.

Candace immediately started to lead others in the field. Able to manage the rough talk and quick pace, she gelled easily with the Emergency Management folks we worked for and kept our staff on schedule and corralled. She worked and worked and worked, somehow also giving CPR training to firemen and working on her nurse practitioner qualifications (she now works full time as a mental health nurse practitioner). Candace said it was helpful to have a lot of work to do to keep her mind off things as her wife was working so hard with COVID patients in the ICU.

Candace's wife was tasked several times to join military medical teams sent to out-of-state hospitals overwhelmed with COVID patients. The teams supplemented staffing until the local resources were enough to take over again. Many military doctors and nurses found themselves battling COVID in hospitals throughout the country.[1] I attended several of their after-action presentations, which described how they stepped into non-ICU wards with large numbers of COVID patients who were very ill and needed ICU-level care. They worked countless hours, often with little sleep. As with other care for patients in the throes of severe COVID-19, they would have ups and downs, good days and bad days, and often after two weeks of working with a patient and their family, the patient would die anyway. Our country's military medical personnel now carry the heavy weight of having their hearts broken in these warlike situations where no bullets flew and no bombs went off. They received little recognition for their amazing work.

Candace and her wife. They are not supposed to be married. I saw them living out Jesus' story. So many self-righteous church people walking on the other side of the road, with the idea of freedom or anti-vaccine sentiment, leaving hundreds of thousands of people to die. And here was this couple, who gave up more than two years of their lives, their comfort, their security, to save people. One became a leader in prevention. The other served her country as the last line of defense to save, when possible, the dying COVID patient.

---

[1] Military Health System, "Military Medical Units Support Civilian Hospitals Strained by COVID-19 Surge," *Health.mil*, February 14, 2022, https://health.mil/News/Articles/2022/02/14/Military-Medical-Units-Support-Civilian-Hospitals-Strained-By-COVID-19-Surge.

Chapter Sixteen: A Place to Serve

Sitting down, Jesus called the Twelve and said, "Anyone who wants to be first must be the very last, and the servant of all."
– Mark 9:35 (NIV)

The most important single element of any corporate, congregational, or denominational culture…is the value system.
– Lyle Schaller[1]

W e desperately needed office space. The first floor of our house, except for the kitchen, had become a medical supply warehouse. On data entry days, we squeezed folding tables between the boxes and entered data. We needed a space that could accommodate all our supplies, the vaccines, and our data team, and we needed it now.

We had projects running in both Pierce County and Lewis County. Because most of our employees were in Pierce, we started our office search there, but we could not find anything that met our needs. Though our Lewis County project was smaller, our responsibilities there were greater since we were not only staffing, but also organizing, supplying, and supervising.

"If we have to have an office…" began Patrick one day as we were driving to a vaccine site. His white Honda was a little small for my six-

---

[1] Lyle Schaller, *Getting Things Done* (Abingdon, 1986), 152.

foot-four frame, but I could still talk, whether or not I could move my legs. "I think it should be in Olympia."

Since leaving the Navy 17 years prior, Jennifer and I lived in the state capital of Olympia, in Thurston County, between Pierce and Lewis. "I do like Olympia," I replied, "but we're short on time, and the places we have looked at so far are not great."

"Justin, the realtor, called yesterday," Patrick said. "He said he just got word about an office opening up after the tenant died of COVID." Patrick put that last part gently. He knew I was still grieving Klara's death.

"That seems a little morbid," I replied

"True. But if he died of COVID, what better way to honor him than to use his office to fight that disease?"

Patrick followed up with Justin, and soon we had a spot in an industrial park that was cheaper than the commercial offices we had looked at. It was ideal for us, with space for the vaccine fridges and supplies, plus a large open area for data entry, and we soon moved in.

Patrick and I knew that an office would take on its own identity with its own culture, obligations, and tasks. We would need someone to manage it. My wife, Jennifer, was handling the finances, a job that was mushrooming as the company grew. Roberta was on the phone from early morning to late evening, scheduling and troubleshooting people's schedules. None of us had the bandwidth to take on the additional responsibility of running an office.

Across the state, the Reinhart family was contemplating a move from Spokane to somewhere west of the mountains. In her job search, Sarah Reinhart typed something backward into the web browser and wound up on our rudimentary website, noticing we were looking for an office manager. In Sarah's words, it was God appointed. The timing was surreal. They were able to move to Olympia, snag an apartment, and start work just as we got the office keys.

At first, Sarah didn't have much to manage: a mostly empty space with a '70s wood-panel theme and a mini-kitchen with a fridge. She was excited to stock the office with supplies, starting with plenty of coffee. If she could have set up IV caffeine bags, I think she would have, but we did have some limits. She kept the place well supplied with many

Keurig choices as well as runs to Starbucks to keep the data entry folks focused and happy.

Sarah Reinhart made the office. She found Bird's Eye Medical, with its need for a fluid approach without much of a blueprint, fresh, exciting, and motivating. She saw it as her mission to do administrative tasks so that she could free other people to do something impactful. She loved to streamline things that would otherwise be time wasters for people. We could not have done what we did without her.

At first, Sarah simply kept the office keys and supported Patrick and me. Roberta mostly worked from home, calling and texting nurses and others at all hours of the day and night as they canceled, called in sick, or rescheduled. The office was buzzing on data days, and a quiet nothing some other days. Always looking to be helpful, Sarah used the slow times to update our web page and make it look more professional.

"Brian, put your desk next to mine," said Carlin, as he and Brian settled in for a day of data entry. "Your brain works better that way. I know it's sensitive and needs to be aligned with the rays coming from the modem."

"Whatever," replied Brian, "hand me that screwdriver, would you? And worry about your own brain."

"Here you go. Watch your fingers. This is real, not a computer game."

"I think I can tell the screw from my fingernail," said Brian. There was a stream of banter between them, almost in a language of their own like twins have sometimes. Others were not always sure they were following the thread, if there was one.

Brian and Carlin were finally able to move out of Roberta's dining room. Though they were at the office much of the time now, Brian and Carlin never quite committed to full-time work. "I don't have a car, and Carlin has to give me a ride," Brian would tell me, as if that explained everything. Carlin was quieter, but when he did talk, especially in front of a group, he would contort his face as he inhaled all the confidence he could. Then out would come something short and witty that set people laughing.

"I need to run to Best Buy for more computers," Sarah said to me casually.

"Just check with Jennifer to make sure our cash flow will allow it," I said. "Cancel that," I added, "I'll ask her." If I sent someone else to ask Jennifer that question, she would want to talk to me first anyway. Sometimes her frugality was a challenge, but she was the one watching the books. And there were several times when cash flow was tight enough that we had to hit pause while we waited for one check or another to come in.

Sarah made runs to Best Buy to buy more computers, mostly Microsoft Surface models. They functioned as tablets in the field, and in the office we added monitors and keyboards to enable multi-screen use, increasing data-entry accuracy.

People started dropping in to talk about their stressors and challenges with Sarah, a safe and nonjudgmental presence. She was the one person not giving shots, hauling vaccines, testing COVID patients, or entering data. She understood how life-giving a listening ear could be to the workers who were busy saving lives. We never knew who would be crying or laughing in her office.

To move the vaccines to the office, we were still waiting for a medical-grade refrigerator. One day after a sleepless night of thawing vaccines, I was at the end of my babysitting tolerance. When Patrick walked in, I growled, "Where's that fridge?" The refrigerator we had ordered from China months before was still held up by supply-chain problems. Patrick dropped what he was doing and by the end of the day had found another one that met our basic criteria: medical grade, physically in a US warehouse, and not currently in customs. According to Murphy's law, that one arrived two days before the one from China we had ordered months before. I still thanked Patrick for his ingenuity, and we could use the two fridges by then anyway, and more would come later. We moved the vaccines in and started training more people.

The person who managed the vaccines in the office had to be smart, detailed, and able to focus. Since vaccines often left the building early and came back late, vaccine managers had to be available before dawn and again late in the afternoon or evening after everyone else had gone home. One reason government agencies did not want to do this work themselves was that it was so hard to find people willing to do this. We were desperate for someone, but would we find them?

At first, we used our portable coolers to transport vaccines. They could be plugged into a car cigarette-lighter port or one of the Yeti batteries. But they took a lot of attention, and the plug-in cords were not the most durable. Some counties were using a more expensive option with Phase Change Materials (PCMs). Pierce County loaned us one of these portable units,[1] which proved easier to use than our plug-in coolers. It consisted of an insulated light canvas box with eight removable green plastic walls, or panels, inside, each about an inch and a half thick and filled with the liquid PCM. The liquid had a freezing point above that of water, so after you set it up correctly by freezing the panels and then putting them at room temperature for 15 minutes, the pack would maintain a temperature of about 4 degrees Celsius for two to three days.

The field vaccine manager was responsible for checking the temperatures at regular intervals. After each trip out of the office, by regulation, we printed out the temperatures for the day and collected them for the state. Any time the vaccine went out of its accepted temperature range, we would have to put that batch aside (still cooled) until the manufacturer advised us whether or not the vaccine could still be used. Only once or twice did we have to discard a few vaccines because they got too warm for too long.

As our mass vaccination work in Pierce County hummed along, we kept hiring and training nurses and administrative support staff. The Pierce County Department of Emergency Management had mass vaccination at the Puyallup fairgrounds, but to ensure access they also chose rural spots and various sites around the city: outside high schools on non-school days, large church parking lots (when the churches were willing), transit centers, and many other locations to do a one-day event or a series of vaccination events. The county's logistics team was amazing, with many from various departments pulling together to make these events happen.

As more vaccines became available, the county pushed to get more and more out at each event. This meant hiring more nurses and getting

---

[1] From the Canadian Company TempArmour.

them trained and organized. Another company purchased its own super-freezer (-80 degrees Celsius) to assist with the supply of Pfizer vaccines to Pierce County. We were already supplying Pfizer to Lewis County (with the help of St. Peter Hospital and their super-freezer in Olympia), but we had not yet been able to buy one of these freezers ourselves. This was no time for competitive secrets, so I asked our crew to help the other company with their certification process and with the protocols and management of the Pfizer vaccine. Once again, our pharmacist, Dr. Rachel Loukas, was very helpful.

Ellen Lenk, the finance officer from Pierce County Emergency Management, would periodically meet with the contract companies like ours on short notice:

"There are more vaccines out there now," Ellen said accusingly. "We need to ratchet it up."

"We are stretched way too thin with the EMS folks and logistics," someone from the county responded, in a voice borrowed from a union meeting. "Overtime is way up. Can we get some more people contracted for this?" Colorful language filled the room as tensions rose.

"We have nurses, and we can increase our numbers working," Patrick said confidently. The head of another small staffing agency agreed. They both knew that their own scheduling folks would probably quit if they heard even half the promises.

"You can't hire people quickly enough," the operations leader chimed in. "You need to add hours to the people you already have."

After the meeting, Patrick told me they were extending hours at the Puyallup fairgrounds, which included a very long stretch for the nurses. I was opposed to this, so we put our nurses in two shorter shifts instead. I had been on the line giving vaccines. I knew from experience how hard it was to give shots in the cold and wet, even for eight to 10 hours at a time, much less longer hours with darkness added. They did try it, but it was unsustainable, and the strategy was shelved.

The relationship between the various county departments was understandably strained by COVID. Verbal jabs and criticisms were common, but in the end, what you saw was people getting vaccines on a mass scale with a high degree of safety and quality. Every time I was at one of the Pierce County events, I marveled at what motivated people working together can achieve.

Ellen is a natural leader, and her skills and doggedness were key to the county's work. She spread out the contracted work to various companies and had high expectations. Saying no to extended nursing hours in one shift may have been the only "no" we gave her.

As for myself, I sometimes wondered what kind of doctor I had become. There was no specialty for my combination of roles, no roadmap for me to follow.

Chapter Seventeen: Doctor of What?

She sets about her work vigorously;
Her arms are strong for her tasks.
She sees that her trading is profitable,
And her lamp does not go out at night.
— Proverbs 31:17–18 (NIV)

There was only this perfect sympathy of movement, of turning this earth
of theirs over and over to the sun, this earth which formed their home
and fed their bodies and made their gods.
— Pearl S. Buck[1]

I t was Monday morning, and I woke up without the alarm at 5 AM. While before COVID, I had needed the alarm, now I no longer bothered setting it. The first thing I noticed was pressure in my chest. I internally sorted it quickly into the non-dangerous category—from knowing I have things I haven't finished or need to start. I rolled out of bed quietly so as not to wake Jennifer. A quick bit of peanut butter on toast while I looked at Jesus's Sermon on the Mount in Matthew 5: "Blessed are the meek." I can carry that phrase today.

I checked my email and replied to my hospice boss: Yes, I can talk about COVID vaccines to the hospice nurses on Thursday morning. He was astonished that some nurses still wouldn't take the vaccine, even

---

[1] Pearl S. Buck, *The Good Earth* (Reader's Digest, 1992), 24.

though they went from nursing homes to assisted living to home settings and could spread the virus to so many vulnerable patients. But my job was to engage and encourage; I was not tasked to enforce. I recalled what my seminary professor told me: "Paul, you get angry when you see what needs to be done. Instead of anger, use what you see to motivate you." That would be the meek approach. I am taking small steps.

I filled out a couple of pending death certificates and looked over my schedule for the week. Monday and Tuesday, I would concentrate on Bird's Eye Medical. The rest of the week, hospice would get priority. No hospital shifts this week.

I started preparing for our Tuesday evening staff meeting on Zoom, pulling up graphs of the current status of COVID in the US: how many deaths per day, how many cases, what vaccines are approved.[1] Any changes to our protocols? I would make sure our folks knew how to access their pay stubs from the online portal. I emailed Patrick, Jennifer, and Roberta: what did they need me to announce? I felt bad making hard-working people join an evening meeting, but years later, people who worked for us would tell me that those online meetings were so helpful, motivating them through that difficult time. Perhaps I had learned from the Navy how to drone on and on to comfort people.

I looked at the clock: Darn it! Already 7:15 AM! I rushed out the door to head to the office. As I started the car, Roberta called, and I put her on speakerphone. "Dr. Bunge, sorry to bother you, but Patrick hates when I call him too early, and someone called in sick who was supposed to be in Lewis County today. Kylie wondered if we could pull Wendy from the office to help. She already said yes, and so did Sarah. Just wanted to check with you." Roberta had already solved her problem, just wanted my sign-off since our Lewis County scheduler recently quit. We needed to hire a scheduling manager for Lewis County soon! Had Patrick posted that job?

"Of course, that's fine," I replied to Roberta.

"Oh, one more thing, Dr. Bunge. Someone who just graduated from

---

[1] The Johnson and Johnson received emergency use authorization at the end of February 2021 ("COVID-19 Timeline").

Washington State University applied for a scribe job. She'll be in the office today for orientation. She seems quite sharp. You might want to talk to her about managing the vaccines."

"Good to know. Thank you, Roberta! You are always looking out for me!"

At the office, Sarah greeted me as she did everyone: with a wide, reassuring smile and warm words to match. We had five minutes in the office together where I mentioned Jesus and the meekness verse while she sipped her Starbucks latte. She knew I was not meek, at least not in a group. Did she know the hole inside me where self-confidence was supposed to be installed? Did she know that my hard work and my perceived assurance were acting as a veneer?

She was excited to show me her latest update for our web page. It was so much more than we had before she came. As I pulled out my to-do list, Brandon, the vaccine manager for that day, came in. "Sarah," he said, "I forgot to charge my cell. Can people text you when they're bringing vaccines in, and then you let me know?"

"Of course," Sarah agreed. Since we had expanded our office staff, sometimes it frustrated me how much she was willing to do for others. Patrick and I both felt like we could use her undivided help more, but at the same time, we admired her attitude.

Brandon turned to give me a smile. "Dr. Bunge, sorry to bother you…" I laughed inside again. My friend and Navy colleague Dr. Rick Sams would say that the doctor's role in this world is to be interrupted. What disease do people schedule anyway? And this was the second person today to apologize.

"I was wondering," Brandon said, "the FedEx tracking system says a box of vaccines arrived two days ago, but I haven't seen it. I can find the supply kits but not the vaccines."

Sarah and I looked at each other wide-eyed, our hearts dropping. Those vaccines were gold, so many people wanted them. More than that, they were saving lives. Had we misplaced them? Were they in the supply room? Would we have to throw them out because they had gotten too warm?

"I'll work on this," I told Sarah. "Keep Patrick busy if he starts looking for me." I knew Patrick had been in a meeting with Ellen yesterday and he was itching to talk to me about it. He would get to the office in half an hour or so, but meanwhile, we needed to get to the bottom of the missing shots.

The vaccine distribution around the country was impressive, a tribute to American shipping companies, the foresight of CDC planners, and an infusion of federal dollars.[1] Before shipping, the CDC and HHS estimated what supply would be available and coordinated with the states on how many doses were to go where. The companies then coordinated with UPS and FedEx.[2] We requested our doses online after talking to the counties, and when approved, we tracked the shipments with FedEx. Each box came with a temperature monitoring system, which we checked on arrival. FedEx delivered our vaccines, and UPS picked up the empty cold storage boxes for use later.

I verified that the supply boxes had arrived as Brandon had said. Someone else had been on duty for vaccines the last few days, but there were no new boxes in the fridge or freezer. What had happened to those vaccines?

Sarah popped her head in the door: "Patrick says you wanted to talk to the new hire."

"Oh yeah, I'll be right there," I told Sarah. "Brandon, keep looking."

I pretended I wasn't distracted by lost vaccines as I greeted a young woman named Kiersten Holguin. I showed her the logbook we used to track the vaccines and the several fridges we had now. I went over how the vaccines worked and some of the rules. She was not scared away and picked things up fast. Could she be our first full-time vaccine manager in the office?

Brandon came in with a new vaccine box, Moderna this time. As Brandon transferred the batch to our freezer, I pointed out to Kiersten

---

[1] Chad Bown and Thomas Bollyky, "How COVID-19 vaccine supply chains emerged in the midst of a pandemic," *The World Economy* 45, no. 2 (2021): 468–522, https://doi.org/10.1111/twec.13183.
[2] Cat Ferguson and Karen Hao, "This is how America gets its vaccines," *MIT Technology Review*, January 27, 2021, https://www.technologyreview.com/2021/01/27/1016790/covid-vaccine-distribution-us/.

that the shipment's listed "expiratory date" was only to be considered a placeholder—a glitch in the system put the printed dates many years in the future. We had to look up the actual date online with the manufacturer for each shipment.

Later, I asked Patrick if he had heard about a missing package. He said he had no idea but wanted to talk to me. "Someone left a message on my cell phone yesterday," Patrick started. "I wasn't sure what they wanted—they were talking about leapfrog shots."

"Was it Ellen?" I asked. What did she have for us now, and how much load could the company and my marriage take? We already needed a bigger office and more staff, and some of our managers needed time off.

"No, it didn't sound like Pierce County," Patrick replied. "I wondered if it was a crank call, someone accusing us of giving someone double shots. Not everyone is happy with us giving COVID vaccines." Yes, we had a few hecklers at the mass vaccination sites, but people were lining up voluntarily, even excitedly, to get shots.

"Wait a minute," I said. "I think Dr. Biggerstaff mentioned that phrase." I reminded Patrick how Lewis County asked us to give vaccinations in group homes and other facilities where it was difficult for the residents to get to the mass vaccination sites. Dr. Biggerstaff and Marshall found that taking the whole team at once to a small facility was inefficient. Those giving the vaccines had to wait until the people doing the paperwork were finished. Getting consent often took longer with this population since family members would often have to be contacted. To confront this challenge, they divided the team in half: the first group worked on consent forms and other paperwork, and then moved on to the next facility, while the second group administered the shots. There might be as few as two people in each group, depending on the size of the facilities. They called this the leapfrog method.

As we were discussing, we could hear Sarah talking to someone at the front doorway. "Just go down three doors. That's the machine shop you are looking for." A woman carrying a package thanked her and walked away. I jumped up with an idea. "Brandon, come with me," I called. "Kiersten, you can come, too." We marched three doors down and entered the machine shop's lobby. A middle-aged man with a goatee and a vine tattoo on his neck asked, "Can I help you folks?"

"Did you happen to get a box addressed to Bird's Eye Medical?" I asked, scanning the room. Brandon pointed to the far-right corner where several boxes sat against the back wall, including the package that the delivery woman had just been holding. The addresses in our complex could be confusing.

"I don't remember anything like that," Mr. Goatee said, as he sorted some parts on the counter.

"Do you mind if we look at the packages in the corner?" I asked. He didn't mind and walked us to the back.

"Here it is, Dr. Bunge!" Brandon exclaimed. It had been there for three days. Would the vaccines still be good? We thanked Mr. Goatee and asked him politely to let us know if it happened again.

Back in our vaccine room, we opened the box. The temperature gauge showed it had stayed within an acceptable range. One problem solved.

Perhaps it doesn't sound as exciting as visiting patients in their hospital beds, and it certainly was a different kind of work. But I knew this was what I was supposed to be doing at that time: finding boxes, running payroll, sustaining and growing a system to keep the vaccines going out, as well as seeing patients.

It was time for lunch, and Patrick and I walked down the street to the taco truck.

"You know how we have been struggling to find people to manage the vaccines in the office?" I asked.

"Of course. Brandon wants to get back out in the field. And Nathan is going back to school. We thought getting an office would solve this problem, but the problem remains."

"It's an odd role that we are trying to fill. Manage a pharmacy, but not really a pharmacy because it only has one type of medication, and they are not given to the patients there. A warehouse, but more than a warehouse, because we are thawing the vaccines and sorting them and putting them with supplies to go out."

"That is why we are trying to train people, but they have to be ready to learn fast and work hard," observed Patrick.

"I am very impressed with Kiersten, though I just met her today.

Perhaps she will be the unicorn we have been looking for."

"I hope so," said Patrick, sounding encouraging.

"So, what was the leapfrog issue all about, since we are using animal metaphors today?"

"I called that number back since you verified it wasn't a prank call," Patrick said. "It was the state Department of Health. They're interested in what we were doing, so I got Dr. Biggerstaff and Marshall back on the phone as well. The health department has a team giving shots in the Seattle area to the same types of smaller facilities that we have been, and they were very excited to talk to our leapfroggers. I think this might turn into something more."

Sure enough, this led to another contract with the state for mobile vaccinations, and we put Marshall Bishop in charge. We didn't think they would have that much work for him, and they didn't for a while. But by this time, as a matter of quality control, we had learned not to take on a new project unless we had a leader for that project, even if it didn't need that much attention at first. Sometimes a project didn't go very far, and the leader would be frustrated. Little did we know that our mobile team project would grow into our biggest program, serving tens of thousands of people throughout the state, and what other roles Marshall Bishop would grow into.

Chapter Eighteen: How to Get It Done

The beginning of wisdom is this: Get wisdom.
Though it cost all you have, get understanding.
                              – Proverbs 4:7 (NIV)

If there is no struggle, there is no progress.
                              – Frederick Douglas[1]

H ow were we supposed to teach our staff about COVID vaccines, especially the staff members without any medical experience? How could we do this safely and effectively, so that we could supplement the work force as much as possible without just pulling nurses from where they were already in short supply? I had taught plenty of people in the past, including medical students, Navy corpsmen, medical residents, and many others, but this challenge was unique, and I would need help.

As I gave a vaccine lecture to Kiersten and another new hire, I remembered teaching clinic workers about Ebola safety measures in Liberia during the outbreak in 2014. The process started with protocols and guidelines from the World Health Organization (WHO) and the Liberia Department of Health. Our organization, Medical Teams International (MTI), had public health professionals review these and

---

[1] Frederick Douglas, *Frederick Douglass on Slavery and the Civil War: Selections from his Writings* (Dover Publications: 2003), 42.

come up with a training curriculum. Then teams would visit the clinics around Monrovia to teach, adapting to the various situations they found, and giving feedback to the clinic managers. I mostly went with these teams, but also reported back to headquarters. I gave lectures to the teams, especially regarding the medical reasons behind decisions made by the leaders in the area. For example, focus on where blood might have contaminated something in the clinic, since transmission was through contact with blood and body fluids.

For training our workers in COVID and vaccinations, we also relied on input and guidelines from experts at the CDC, the state Department of Health, vaccine companies, and the literature. From there, we made our own protocols and updated them internally as more data became available. As we worked with various groups, we adapted. I focused on the "why" once again, reading and educating as we went along. Later, we added a quality committee and feedback mechanisms that were very helpful to ensure high quality at each stage.

As I drew on the whiteboard (my writing is messy and my drawings are horrible, so I am not sure it helps anyone but me), my audience sat attentively:

"There are three vaccines, two using mRNA in nanoparticles. Do you know what they do in the body?"

"Somehow, they trigger the immune system," offered Kiersten.

"Yes," I continued, "whether it is manufactured mRNA or a weakened other virus, they all get some RNA into the cell. The cell makes part of the COVID protein, and the body then reacts to that protein. This is how the body learns to resist COVID."

"But doesn't that mean the patient will always have COVID DNA in them?" asked the other new hire.

"No. Messenger RNA is the way the body's DNA signals the cell to make proteins. The process doesn't go backwards, so the DNA is not changed." As I talked about the new vaccines, I mentioned more about the Moderna and Pfizer shots. "These small lipid sacs that carry the mRNA are made by nanotechnology. This is the reason we don't shake the vial or tap the syringe, because that could disrupt the microspheres. But tapping the syringe to get rid of bubbles is a habit that is hard to break; the nurses are so used to it. This is also the answer to why we don't drive the vaccines too far once thawed, since the vibrating vehicle is also an issue in disrupting the nanoparticles."

I went on to tell them you can't leave the refrigerator door open very long, or it will warm up too much. In the vaccine room, we traced out the wires on the battery backup system so they understood the switches and could troubleshoot if needed.

At least half of our Tuesday staff meetings on Zoom were education focused. I talked about what to do if someone accidentally pokes themself with a needle after giving a vaccine. I spoke about how masks work, how the immune system takes a while to respond to the vaccine. Others updated the staff on protocols and changes.

For the workers in the field giving shots, I asked our nurse, Candace, for help. As usual, she made a mildly sarcastic comment in reply, then agreed. Some training she could do online, but we both agreed there needed to be hands-on work, some of it before they could see the patients. After that, she would supervise them with the actual patients in the field. But where to do the pre-patient hands-on training? Before we had an office, we considered renting a training space, but ultimately, Candace had most people come to her house. I was surprised at this, since she and her wife were nervous about having outsiders there. But once she had made a decision, Candace could be quite stubborn, even with herself. Trainees got to meet their zealous Labrador retrievers, and if they could handle them and Candace herself, they were well on their way. Once we had the office, the training moved there.

Now that we had smaller teams going out, some with the state contract and some otherwise, more clinical questions were coming my way. I knew I needed some backup, even though there were not that many actual calls. Sometimes I was working at the hospital or out on a hospice visit and hard to reach. Questions included what to do when someone showed up for their second AstraZeneca shot that was not approved or available in the USA, after getting the first overseas. A patient had COVID last week or last month—when should they get a shot? Some people tried to inappropriately get extra shots. One person insisted that the nurse not call the ambulance, even though they were having a significant reaction to the vaccine in the school gym where our event was taking place.

Dr. Joel Abbott, who had worked with me at the Army hospital and in my rural health project, helped out, as did Dr. Biggerstaff, and I made a call schedule.

"I found another couple of filing cabinets up in Tacoma on Facebook Marketplace," said Patrick one morning at the office as I looked up bleary eyed and Sarah listened intently over her Frappuccino. "I think I can fit them in my hatchback one by one." This was after we started with Lewis County but were still using the paper-only method at Pierce County.

"What are we doing with all these filing cabinets?" I wondered out loud. "We are only a small corner of this country. Can you imagine how much storage space the country is dedicating to this exercise right now? There must be a hundred million paper forms already to store for several years. Where's the electronic medical record for this?"

Patrick and I had predicted the computer program Solv would do much better than the state's choice, PrepMod. How wrong we were. We were able to compare, since Pierce County signed up for Solv and we used PrepMod in Lewis County. PrepMod worked very well, as Kylie and Erika had predicted. Meanwhile in Pierce County, long after PrepMod was up and running, Solv had yet to become functional. They could not get their data to accurately upload into the state system, and even after implementation, we had many more errors to fix in our Pierce County work than we did in Lewis County. At several events we did double work, as we entered the data into Solv, but then had to re-enter it manually when Solv failed to transfer the data as planned.

I later learned that PrepMod had been built on decades of work with vaccines in lower-income communities.[1] They had worked out the bugs in the interface with the states' quirky databases long before COVID started. This system was made by a creative public health worker, Tiffany Tate, who during the 2009 flu season had the same frustration we had with data input. Tate tried to work with the CDC early in the COVID pandemic, but the federal government instead contracted with a large corporation. Their expensive program did not work well at all,

---

[1] Sheryl Stolberg, "Immunization Expert Accuses CDC and Deloitte of Stealing Her Idea," *New York Times*, February 7, 2021, https://www.nytimes.com/2021/02/06/us/politics/coronavirus-vaccines.html.

and many states wound up paying Tate for her program, PrepMod.[1]

We did our best to help Pierce County with the Solv program. Several times we assigned our very capable Madi Hubble to troubleshoot issues and discuss strategies when the Solv reps were on site in Pierce County. She persisted and helped them despite one particularly difficult day when a computer programmer was condescending and inappropriate. Some people apparently do not feel secure in the world without stepping on someone else.

Speaking of stepping on others, I was surprised and saddened when I saw women and minorities treated poorly as we worked in various communities. The few times we saw this among our own employees, we tried our best to intervene. But what were we supposed to do when we saw something wrong, but it had to do with a different company or agency that we were working with but had no significant say over?

There was a security guard who didn't work for us but was assigned to help us with a project. Several women said he made them feel afraid and was odd in his conversation with them. Patrick and I talked about the situation. If he had worked for us, we would have fired him. But he didn't, and when we brought it up with our partner organization, we were told it was too politically difficult to let him go. We decided to bear with it and steer people away from him the best we could. I am not sure that was the right choice, and it still bothers me. We were trying to make things happen to save lives and didn't want to rock the boat. But isn't that a kind of justification that perpetuates the problem?

Why not just treat people decently, try to work together, whatever your gender, orientation, color, religion, or whatever else? You don't have to be like the other person or agree with them on everything, as long as you have some common goal and treat people with respect. Some people seem to have this inner need to step on others. Individuals, groups, countries. I have seen it too many times.

Patrick and I noticed what others were reporting. Minority groups were generally not getting vaccinated as much, for many reasons. From

---

[1] Cat Ferguson, "What went wrong with America's $44 million vaccine data system?" *MIT Technology Review*, January 30, 2021, https://www.technologyreview.com/2021/01/30/1017086/cdc-44-million-vaccine-data-vams-problems/.

the beginning, we did outreach work with minority community groups, an effort that would continue.

"Dr. Bunge, did you even know I was black when you hired me?" Marshall Bishop asked one day when he, Patrick, and I were sitting down together at the park benches outside the office for some fast food since we had missed dinner. As the days get longer and the weather gets warmer and less rainy, the Pacific Northwest has some of the best weather in the world.

"Frankly, I had no idea," I replied. "We didn't even use Zoom. I just called you on the phone as I ran through my long list of logistics candidates."

Marshall smiled. "I didn't think so," he said. And that was that. I was blessed to have this motivated and capable man working for me. When he was asked by one county's public health department to stop giving them ideas, they lost out on some good COVID-fighting coordination, probably because they couldn't see past his skin color.

Many times during the pandemic, I thought back to my weeks in Liberia during the Ebola crisis. It was a war against a horrible virus, where brave medical workers and the citizens of the three countries fought hard to contain it and keep it from spreading to the whole world. In the end, just over 11,000 people died of Ebola during those three years. People of a darker hue saved the world by their hard work and sacrifice. I remember distinctly how relatively little help was sent to West Africa by other countries during that time, though the technology available would have saved lives and reduced the risk of spread.[1] It seemed to me at that time that a black life was internationally seen as much less valuable than a white one.

During its major peaks, COVID killed more people per week in the US than Ebola did in all three years of that crisis. Yet somehow, despite so many deaths and the dramatic effect of the vaccine, an odd idea was spreading: that taking the shot was not worth the risk. We would soon

---

[1] Helen Branswell, "MSF Call for Military Help with Ebola Response Shows Outbreak's Severity," *Global News—The Canadian Press*, September 3, 2014, https://globalnews.ca/news/1540612/msf-call-for-military-help-with-ebola-response-shows-outbreaks-severity.

be shocked by how extensive this perception had become.

Chapter Nineteen: Where Are the Rest?

And [Jesus] was amazed at their unbelief.
> *– Mark 6:6a (NASB)*

All happy families are alike; each unhappy family is unhappy in its own way.

> *– Leo Tolstoy, in the opening to Anna Karenina[1]*

B y May of 2022, Bird's Eye Medical had over 150 employees working in four counties at mass vaccination sites (we were supplying nurses to Clark County and Thurston County also by this time). We had smaller teams in facilities, going to the houses of people who couldn't get out, and at community events across western Washington. We were doing outreach to various minority groups. We were settling into a regular rhythm. Pierce County started using the large entertainment venue, the "Tacoma Dome," to get the other half of the county vaccinated, and we tapped Jennifer "JJ" Jewitt as our nurse lead for that project.

Suddenly, the mass vaccinations dried up. We went from several thousand shots per day to a hundred or two at most. We knew we had gotten through only about half the adults, and I knew from my work at

---

[1] Leo Tolstoy, *Anna Karenina* (Barnes & Nobles Classics), 5.

the hospitals that it was primarily unvaccinated people who were still dying by the hundreds per day throughout the country. But the lines were gone, and we were left standing there. If I hadn't seen it, I would not have believed it. As it was, I was frustrated beyond belief. Here is your lifesaving vaccine! Why won't you take it?

Other people working in mass vaccinations reported the same experience. There was a single day when they noticed a dramatic drop, like the water had been cut off and the faucet only gurgled. One day, people were clamoring, begging, and traveling long distances so they could get the vaccine quicker. The next day, it slowed to a trickle.

What happened? Every adult American who has gone to school has been taught about infections and how to prevent them. It has been several generations since any significant percentage of our population has doubted the germ theory. Every high school in the country has microscopes. It has been nearly a hundred years since the invention of the electron microscope, which made viruses visible. The effectiveness of vaccines in preventing disease has been historically proven beyond possible doubt. Yet, despite our familiarity with what causes disease and the effectiveness of vaccines, many people in this country decided for a myriad of reasons to refuse the no-cost vaccines that could have saved their lives and prevented transmission of a virus that was still killing between 600 and 4,000 Americans every single day.[1]

The reasons that people did not take their COVID shots were so varied and unpredictable that even attempting to sort the explanations gives the impression that there is a rhyme or reason when there may be none at all. The best I can do is list the reasons that people gave me and look into the literature on what has been called vaccine hesitancy.

Some people simply hate being poked by needles. They reminded

---

[1] The effectiveness of the COVID vaccine in preventing disease and death was confirmed in several studies besides the ones that proved their effectiveness prior to approval. The following study compared county vaccine rates and showed that people in counties with higher vaccination rates were hospitalized and died less: John McLaughlin et al., "County-level vaccination coverage and rates of COVID-19 cases and deaths in the United States: An ecological analysis," *The Lancet Regional Health—Americas* 9 (May 2022), https://doi.org/10.1016/j.lana.2022.100191.

me of the brave, muscular soldiers and sailors I cared for in the military who passed out when they were getting ready for a shot or a blood draw. They could take a bullet but not a needle. Others believed the vaccine was safe and effective, yet still felt afraid, like someone who knows airplanes are safe yet panics when even thinking about flying.

Some said they opposed the COVID vaccine for religious reasons. They cited either an aversion to the use of cells derived from aborted fetuses[1] or that they thought belief in God was enough to prevent disease, and taking a vaccine would be a sign of doubt. For most people citing religious concerns, it seemed to me that their actual decision was based on politics or fear or something else, and the religious terminology was added later.

Some people objected to vaccines because of a certain political mindset: because the government promoted something was enough to say "no" to it. Some people were convinced that the COVID pandemic was a myth, or that the response was an overreaction, that there never was a serious danger in the first place.

Some people decided the COVID vaccine involved unacceptable risks for them relative to their benefit. COVID vaccines do have risks, some of which were not clear when they first came out, like many medications. Examples of these include the mRNA vaccines giving a small increased risk of heart inflammation (myocarditis), especially in young males. Women who took the Johnson and Johnson vaccine had a small increased risk of blood clots.[2] To add to this, younger people had

---

[1] A cell line derived from aborted fetal tissue was used in one stage of testing of the mRNA vaccines, but it was not used in the manufacture of the vaccines. Another cell line derived from aborted fetal tissue was used in the manufacture of the Johnson and Johnson vaccine. These two cell lines from the 1970s and 1980s are used in testing and development in many areas of medicine currently, and it is very difficult to avoid any connection with them completely. Most ethicists, including conservative-leaning ones opposed to abortion, consider it ethical to take these vaccines, including the Johnson and Johnson one. See the Christian Medical Association Position Statement on Vaccines and Immunizations for further info: https://cmda.org/policy-issues-home/position-statements/.

[2] "Coronavirus Disease 2019 (COVID-19) Vaccine Safety," *CDC*, December 20, 2024, https://www.cdc.gov/vaccine-safety/vaccines/covid-19.html.

less risk to their own health from a COVID infection than the elderly.

I heard a whole gamut of conspiracy theories, such as the claim that the vaccines cause infertility, that they alter DNA, that they implant a microchip under your skin, and even if those aren't exactly what happens, the vaccines are the result of a coordinated cabal of child-abusing leftists who want to take away your freedoms and bring many other evils, so they are simply bad. Of course, none of these statements are true, but it was difficult to know even how to start to respond to them because they are so odd and extreme.

The person who starts a falsehood, such as that vaccines cause autism or infertility, is using their creativity without the balance of rationality. When someone makes a random claim about vaccines that is not based on reality, the doctor or nurse has no answer—at first. It takes time to look for research that addresses that particular issue (if the literature exists), analyze the known data, and then formulate an answer that addresses the questioner's concern. Suppose your friend tells you your headaches are due to carpenter ants in your walls. You invest the time and energy and expense to remove enough drywall to be confident that your house is not infested, but your headaches persist. Then your friend says, "Well, your headaches must be caused by the powerlines across the street. You need to move." You quickly learn that your well-meaning and creatively thinking friend may well be wasting your time.

The current version of Harrison's textbook of medicine looks at several things to gauge how likely people are to take vaccines.[1] Complacency when disease incidence is low is a factor. Confidence in the safety and effectiveness of the vaccine, and in the health care system in general, is important. Most of those who study this area consider that the COVID years occurred just as other social and cultural trends were making misinformation more available and acceptable. Discrimination contributed to hesitation in minority and marginalized communities. The degree of politicization surrounding COVID vaccines is remarkable and clearly contributed to the hesitancy.

---

[1] Julie Bettinger and Hana Mitchell, "Chapter 3: Vaccine Opposition and Hesitancy," *Harrison's Principles of Internal Medicine*, 21e, ed. Loscalzo et al. (McGraw-Hill Education, 2022).

The other major challenge is that we are often mistaken when we think that our decisions are all based primarily on rationality. As shown by Jonathan Haidt[1] and others, our emotions have much more control over our decisions than we give them credit for. We are only "beginning to understand the complex interplay between emotion, affect, and reason that is wired into the human brain and essential to rational behavior, [and] the challenge before us is to think creatively about what this means for managing risk."[2]

Someone can explain rationally their reason for not taking the vaccine. As a doctor, I can reply rationally to the concern and present arguments. But neither the patient's nor my own rational mind is completely in charge of our halves of the discussion. For example, behind someone's stated reason could be fear of a relative experiencing a severe complication or death from a COVID shot. These are powerful emotions. All the reasoning in the world may not sway that person, and the wise doctor will be careful how and when to even raise the issue.[3]

I remember when my father died. My grief just before and after he left us was quite sharp, and I could not think or act as I probably would have without that grief. Could the pain and trauma of going through COVID and an unusual behavior, such as rejecting lifesaving medication, be related? A sort of grief reaction? Denial and anger have been described as part of the grieving process.[4] Would addressing this help? And could addressing our national grief help us heal as a nation now?

If people were not going to come in, it was time to shut down the

---

[1] Jonathan Haidt, *The Righteous Mind: Why Good People Are Divided by Politics and Religion* (Pantheon Books, 2012).
[2] Paul Slovic et al., "Risk as Analysis and Risk as Feelings: Some Thoughts about Affect, Reason, Risk, and Rationality," *Risk Analysis* 24, no. 2 (2004): 311–322, https://doi.org/10.1111/j.0272-4332.2004.00433.x.
[3] For further discussion on the importance of decision-making in medicine and the various factors involved, I strongly recommend Dr. Francis Collins's recent book: *The Road to Wisdom: On Truth, Science, Faith, and Trust* (Little, Brown and Company, 2024).
[4] Elizabeth Kübler-Ross, *On Death and Dying* (Simon & Schuster, 1970).

mass vaccination sites. Smaller numbers could be served by drugstores. I was surprised when the state asked us to send small teams of vaccinators to sites throughout the community. I thought that this was going to be a waste of time and money: if someone can't bother to go through the very simple process of the drive-through, how was bringing the vaccine to the grocery store or the community event going to work? But it did work. When we went to where the people were and took time to answer their questions, many people got vaccinated who had not previously.

Some venues brought better results than others. "Sunday, we were at a Catholic church after Mass," said Marshall. "That's one of the best places to set up. The priest had asked us to come, and we gave 40 shots after each service."

"What about the Seahawks game?" asked Patrick. He knew that one of our vaccine teams had set up at the stadium the previous Sunday.

"Well, it was fun to be there, that's for sure," Marshall replied, looking away.

"But how many shots?"

"Hm...two I think?" Marshall admitted.

Jennifer and I had figured that one out early on at the local high school. When we set up in the cafeteria on the weekend and invited the community, they came. But showing up at the Friday night high school football game? Nobody wanted to get a vaccine there—they were too excited about the score and the band and the romantic dramas playing out. We set up at the Cambodian festival outside a Buddhist temple in Tacoma and waited for people to filter by after they bought their hot pepper plants. Many stopped to chat and then get a vaccination. They felt comfortable and honored. A naturopath from Seattle called us about COVID vaccines, once he figured out how hard it would be to order his own, and we coordinated a small team to go to his office. We did this with other clinics as well, since most adult doctors' offices don't store vaccines. A patient usually trusts their doctor. If that doctor asks the patient to get the vaccine, and has it in the office for them, that helps.

Farmers markets, county fairs, almost everything we could think of we tried: sometimes it worked and sometimes it didn't. I spent an afternoon at a large brewery in Seattle: only a few takers. Again, the football game wasn't the right vibe, even if it was only on TV.

The transition from mass vaccination to sending small teams all over the state required extensive organization of travel, hotels, vaccine storage, and especially coordination with community contacts. We started on the west side of the state, but later we were sending people over the mountains as well.

I am still amazed at the refusal of COVID vaccines, which between 2021 and 2023 could have prevented between 200,000 and 320,000 American deaths, or more.[1] If I was on my own facing this shocking reality as the mass vaccination sites closed, I think I would have been paralyzed, with my visceral response to preventable deaths. But I was not alone. I had an amazing team. Rather than being stopped by this frustration, we pivoted, as we had before.

But was my vision and my team's motivation enough to keep Jennifer and me working together? We were feeling our relationship fray with the long days, stress, constant changes, and our different approaches to business in general. We were managing, but we missed our times together, holidays, talking about something other than work. Answers were short and crisp much too frequently. Our emotional bank account was going into the red.

---

[1] Katherine Jia et. al., "Estimated preventable COVID-19-associated deaths due to non-vaccination status in the United States," *European Journal of Epidemiology* 38, no. 11 (2023), 1125–1128, https://doi.org/10.1007/s10654-023-01006-3.

Chapter Twenty: Life Test

Plans fail for lack of counsel, but with many advisers they succeed.
— Proverbs 15:22 (NIV)

"After all, I think we can agree without exaggeration or fear of contradiction that the times have changed..."
"It is the business of the times to change, Mr. Halecki. And it is the business of gentlemen to change with them."
— Amor Towles[1]

In August of 2021, the number of COVID infections nationally started rising again. I hoped this would just be minor fluctuations in a new normal, but with so many people not vaccinated, new strains, and school starting in the fall, I feared it spelled trouble.

As restrictions on gatherings were relaxed, our sense of urgency intensified. I wasn't opposed to the changes. What approach the government should take was becoming less and less clear at this stage, as we tried to balance the need for people to get together with the increase in cases and the fact that about half the country was still not vaccinated. With the government's role decreasing, it felt like more responsibility was falling on those of us outside the government. Was there more we could do to save lives?

---

[1] Amor Towles, *A Gentleman in Moscow* (Penguin, 2019), 75.

I talked to my wife, Jennifer. I knew we, as well as our relationship, were strained. But she was strong, and I was motivated. I asked her for another six months at least before we backed off with the company. She agreed, and she meant it. She is not shy to speak her mind. But I also knew her support was weaker than before, and our relationship would be even more challenged.

The most important thing we could do, it seemed to me, was to keep making the vaccines easily available and encourage people to take them. We would keep our high-quality mobile teams going out all over the state. We supported vaccination projects at the shopping malls in Olympia and in Puyallup. I wondered, though, if we could save even more lives by helping with testing.

COVID testing was available both through the regular medical system, though it was still strained and sometimes hard to get, and at easier-to-access sites that did only testing, such as my own county's drive-through site. But Thurston County was talking about closing its site, and I wondered if the usual medical system could take up the slack, especially if there was more need over the next several months. On the other hand, some were arguing that testing was no longer useful. This debate reminded me of my work with HIV in Africa.

In the early 1990s, there was debate among those in healthcare development about whether it was worth the time and effort to support testing for HIV in sub-Saharan Africa. The disease was obviously spreading rapidly and many lives were being lost. But medications were not yet very effective, and essentially inaccessible in Africa. The prevailing opinion was that for an African to know he or she was HIV-positive would only cause that person to be frustrated and confused and pull resources from other medical needs.[1] Some, however, felt that this was merely an instance of wealthy nations telling the Africans that they couldn't handle the truth.

It seemed to me that where testing was done, HIV spread decreased. When people knew they were infected, they behaved differently,

---

[1] R. Baggale et. al., "From caution to urgency: the evolution of HIV testing and counselling in Africa," *Bulletin of the World Health Organization* 90, no. 9 (2012): 652–658B, https://doi.org/10.2471/BLT.11.100818.

whether or not effective treatment was available. Most people who know they are HIV-positive change their behavior in ways that make transmission less likely.

I also believed that if people knew they had COVID, they would behave differently, and most would try to protect other people, even without mandatory isolation. So, even before we had much in the way of specific early treatments and when COVID was still very dangerous, I saw testing as a powerful tool for saving lives.

In this light, with people talking about closing testing sites, I couldn't just sit by and do nothing. I called the county medical director, various clinics around town, and the two hospitals to see what their plans were and if they thought they had capacity to do the extra testing. Some would say, "I don't know if we can provide enough access to testing, and I don't have a crystal ball—do you?" That was bad enough. But then others would say, "We won't need testing because COVID numbers won't go that high anymore," as if they did have a crystal ball. That drove me even crazier. I couldn't understand how medical people could miss the urgency. After all these months, I still hadn't gotten used to it. At our office, people saw the boss walking around frustrated and angry. I struggled to keep that anger flame on the stove and not let it spread.

I called private testing companies. They largely worked off a similar model: the county, a company, or a school pays per test run. But those sources of funding were drying up. I knew we could open our own site and charge the patient's medical insurance, but we would lose money doing it, maybe a lot of money. Patrick and my wife, business minded as they are, thought that was crazy, but they let me investigate it anyway, thinking I would lose interest after a while.

Knowing the Thurston site was closing any day, I caught Patrick as he sat at his computer: "What if we buy a building and use it temporarily for testing? Even if we lose money on testing, the building will be an investment, and the value will probably increase after COVID is over and people go back to the office."

Patrick's eyes came up from his computer and met mine. "Now that might be interesting," he said, leaning back in his chair. The wheels were turning. Within 10 minutes, he made an Excel file with down payment and bank loan considerations, found a real estate agent's number, and calculated what we could afford with potential 10-year returns.

That night, I brought it up with my wife, Jennifer. "We should not bite off more when things are winding down," she said matter-of-factly. She seemed to use the phrase "winding down" quite a bit lately, even though we were hiring more people and planning on a larger office space. Maybe not a good sign. But instead of glaring, she looked to the corner of the room as she tried to hide the fact that she was calculating in her head the same general numbers that Patrick had put into his computer. Why not put some of that money we made to good use, like into a building, before Paul comes up with another scheme to lose it?

Jennifer and I agreed that we should avoid renting if possible. The large ownership groups that rent out commercial space have developed quite the scheme to shift all the risk and costs onto the renter. It has become standard practice for small companies to cover not just rent, but property taxes, maintenance of the building, and all insurance as well (called "the standard triple net lease"). We had run into this when renting our second office space, which is partly what prompted us to consider buying a building for testing.[1]

Patrick, Sarah, and I looked at a building up on the hill near the courthouse. It was quite attractive, with many windows that would make working there more pleasant. There was a circular drive in the back that could function as a drive-through testing site. All three of us were excited.

But the next day, consistent with my tendency to drive people crazy with my back-and-forth thinking, I told Patrick: "You know, after sleeping on it…I have a problem with that building. The storage room

---

[1] It puzzles me that this topic is not more discussed in the peer-reviewed business literature. I only find evidence that shifting these costs onto the renter benefits the investor. No surprise there. Private equity firms pour fortunes into buying these buildings. That system apparently works for big companies who rent buildings en masse for their branches. But it seems a weakness in our economy: stifling creativity when small business owners already are risking their own money (not rolling dice with other people's money like the private equity firms).

is way too small."

"What do you mean?" Patrick asked.

I continued: "Our main job now is mobile vaccination teams. That means we must keep track of not just vaccines and their supplies, but tents, batteries, traffic cones, and more."

"Good point. We have more gear than it looks like. So much is distributed here and there in rental vans and at employees' garages. If we gathered it all back, it wouldn't fit in the office at all." We let that nice building on the hill go to someone else.

Several days later, Patrick said, "There is another building," though he didn't sound excited. "It's the old Greyhound station downtown."

"That's still empty?" I asked. It had been boarded up for a few years.

That day, we drove down to look at the building. I had memories of dropping off our oldest son, David, to catch the bus to college. Eventually, David figured out how to use Facebook to find rides with other students. A lot of people were finding other ways to get around as well, and Greyhound closed many of its stations around the country, including ours.

The building was in bad shape. Boarded up, filthy all around, littered with needles, and painted with graffiti. The building itself is Art Deco style, built in the 1930s. In my mind's eye, I could see it looking great again. The large, covered garage open on both ends would be perfect for drive-through testing. Our real estate agent made inquiries, and it seemed like half the businesses downtown had investigated buying the building at one time or another, but each had hit some sort of snag. Sometimes it was the question of underground contamination. Other times it was that Greyhound was a stiff organization, difficult to navigate.

Greyhound was paying for a guard on site 24 hours per day. They had put up gates on the garage, but they were flimsy and you could easily push through them. When we first showed up to check out the building with the agent, we couldn't find the guard. Eventually, we pushed through the gates ourselves and found him asleep in his truck. It took my pounding multiple times on the windshield to wake him.

In prior attempts at sale, Greyhound had done a thorough asbestos removal, which was good news. We did studies and learned about groundwater, city ordinances, downtown trash pickup, and security systems.

Our real estate agent somehow did what no one else had been able to do, and we got a reasonable deal on the building. Even so, the process dragged on before we could actually move in, so we rented a couple of shipping containers and set them up in the parking lot next door, which we rented temporarily. Between the portable "buildings," tents, and ingenuity of the team, I thought we would be ready to start testing by the beginning of September. Sarah, always wanting to help, set up a credit card payment system.

One day my cell lit up with a call from Angi Swinhart, a nurse whom I had worked with in the small hospital at Elma. She had helped me set up a consult clinic there and coordinate Hepatitis C treatments with the University of Washington (UW).

"Hi, Angi," I answered the call. "I'm on the road between hospice patients right now. How's it going?"

"I'm good, Dr. Bunge." After catching up briefly, Angi continued: "Do you still have any need for me at your company?" I had called her a couple of times when we were so busy with the mass vaccinations, but she had a full work schedule at the time.

"Wow, as it happens, I really need a project manager for my testing site idea," I said, excitedly giving her the quick lowdown. "You have to understand, this is going to be downtown at a derelict building, outside in the rain to start. You will have to help make the plan and then manage the people. And we will be losing money. And it will be temporary. Are you sure you want to do it?"

"Dr. Bunge, if you are involved, it's going to be crazy, but I wouldn't miss it for the world." Angi took the job. She knew me and trusted me. She was also familiar with my tendency to go down rabbit holes and my need to be refocused, and she was able to "manage" me without getting too frustrated.

Which lab could we get to run our tests? We talked to Labcorp and Quest, the two large national labs. They were running COVID tests by then, but the turnaround time was not great. The local hospitals said no. I reached out to the UW and made it through a couple of people but found navigating the bureaucracy difficult. We were running some testing in Lewis County through Labcorp, so we decided to use them and scale up, despite their limitations. The biggest problem was that they would not agree to run tests on people without insurance—we would have to pay for those ourselves if we wanted to do them. I was willing to waive the collection fee for those folks, but when we were already expecting to lose money, how could we pay Labcorp another $100 for each test on people without insurance, or who had given us the wrong info, or whose insurance turned them down for one reason or another? I hated to do it, but I had to say we would only take people with insurance.

The day before we planned to open, one of the people we hired told me I was shooting from the hip and we were not ready. He didn't bother showing up the next day, and we didn't have enough people to move ahead. But he was right, we weren't ready, and we didn't open until later in September. First, we did a trial day, and it went fine. We had someone bring the samples over to the office after the drive-through closed and put them in the box for Labcorp to pick up. Several days later we had results.

We finally opened in late September 2021 in the parking lot. I thought we would be in the building soon, but with so many administrative delays, we had to stay in the parking lot until January. We had enough workers, but turnover was high. Angi and a few others soldiered on, but it wasn't easy. Besides contending with the elements, a significant number of people wandered the area who were either houseless or using drugs or both. We had to clean up human waste, needles, and trash. Some people said they specifically wanted to work downtown. Their tender hearts did not always correlate with enough toughness to make it more than a few days. But eventually, we gathered a cadre of people with that right combination of caring hearts and thick skin.

A few days after our trial run, the UW lab called me back. I had left them messages, knowing of their exceptional work, but I assumed they had moved on and were not interested in our testing site. However, once I connected with the correct team, they said that they could certainly support our site. They would charge insurance, but those without insurance would not be charged. We took the same approach with the collection fees and were able to take whoever showed up. The university sent a driver daily who picked up our samples, and they usually had the results back the next morning, with the notable exception of the Omicron peak which backed everyone up. Dr. Alex Greninger and his team[1] continued the fantastic job they had started early in the pandemic.

How would we register people for testing? We knew the online access program, Solv, had its problems, but we also knew Solv was easy for the patients to use.[2] The UW lab had allowed a computer interface between Solv's system and their lab record system, such that the patient received a text when the lab was complete, and they could log on and find the result.

We soon had a smooth system running with Solv, the UW lab, and my soggy crew. PCR tests were free to the patients (we collected insurance when we could), and we charged $35 by credit card for rapid tests. This encouraged people to get the more accurate PCR test, though if they needed or preferred a rapid test, it was available (rapid tests were not yet over the counter).

We knew people were getting their results, but we wanted to make sure they had more information and access to resources if their tests were positive. We set up a call system for our staff to call patients who were positive for COVID. Little did we know how useful that would be later.

One day there was a shooting a few blocks from our testing site. I drove downtown, and by then the danger appeared to be passed. Nonetheless, I sent everyone home for the rest of the day with pay. They were just too nervous to leave the portable building where they were hiding out. Another day, an angry woman got out of her car to give the staff a lecture about the evils of vaccines. They tried to explain this was only a testing site, but she would not listen, proceeded to throw down

---

[1] See Chapter 3.

[2] What Solv did to effectively allow patients to enter their own core data such as name and date of birth and thus create a medical record was nothing short of revolutionary. It may not seem that important to those outside the medical system, but this approach has been considered absolutely unacceptable for so many years within medicine and electronic medical records.

our signs, and threatened to kill one of our staff members. The police didn't come until much later, complaining of recent state restrictions on police meant to curb overreactions.[1] I tried to set up an on-call system with local security firms, but they were prohibitively expensive and only open to having someone on-site full time, which seemed excessive.

It seemed our downtown testing site felt like a burden not worth the effort, with people walking off the job after a few days of cold and wet and the rough people hanging around. But later, we realized that this was good for the company in many ways. Those who could manage that work could be trusted with more. And the longer we stayed in that location, the more the neighborhood supported us, from the surrounding businesses to the street mental health teams, to the local radio station. People started to feel that this was their Olympia testing site, and that it could be trusted.

Ellen from Pierce County, who had managed our work with mass vaccinations, called us in the fall of 2021. Our contract with Pierce was inactive at the time, since our mobile vaccine clinics were through the state, not the county. But this time, Ellen wanted help with testing. One of the tribes had requested the county's help with COVID testing for workers and others at one of the large casinos. Soon, we had testing up and running there as well, organized by another very capable nurse, Tessa Fitzgerald. There were many cold, rainy days under the tarp for Tessa and her team as they worked at the site of the former casino, which resembled an abandoned construction site, with the flashy new casino next door, complete with a giant video screen on Highway I-5 promoting the latest prize offerings, steak and shrimp, and 1980s rock bands. We were able to open this site to the public as well.

The testing sites around the state that had stayed open and the newly opened sites, like the tribe's, would prove invaluable in the next chapter of COVID: the Omicron surge that started in December of 2021 and lasted several months.

---

[1] Austin Jenkins, "With 12 New Laws, Washington State Joins Movement to Overhaul Policing," *NPR*, May 18, 2021, https://www.npr.org/2021/05/18/997974519/ a-dozen-police-reform-bills-signed-into-law-in-washington-state.

Chapter Twenty-One:
Who Needs Therapy?

And who knows whether you have not come to the kingdom for such a time as this?
— Esther 4:14b (RSV)

Where you live in the world should not determine whether you live in the world.
— Bono[1]

"Where are we going, Daddy?" asked the five-year-old girl in the back seat. "I thought we were getting ice cream."

"We will, honey, we will," answered the muscular black man. "But Daddy has to stop here a minute for work."

"OK, Daddy," was the reply. Ezra Stark wondered at the good nature of his daughter and hoped that when they returned to Olympia, she wouldn't tell her mother he had been working.

This job shouldn't be as challenging as the two deployments to Iraq when I was on active duty, he thought. *I am not around bullets or IEDs or gone for months at a time, but it takes all the brainpower I can muster, and I'm responsible for so many lives!*

---

[1] Bono (lead singer from U2), "My wish: Three actions for Africa," TED Talk, February 2005, https://www.ted.com/talks/bono_my_wish_three_actions_for_africa.

Ezra pulled the SUV into the parking lot at Yard Birds in Centralia. Yard Birds started as a military surplus store after World War II and grew into a local icon and powerhouse retailer with a large department store.[1] National chains like Kmart and Walmart meant the huge building had gone through several attempts at relevance since then, and most of it at this time was occupied by a large flea market where Spanish was heard more than English. That was where Bird's Eye Medical had set up on a Saturday morning to offer COVID vaccines, in partnership with the local Hispanic community organization and the state's Care-a-Van outreach program. Ours was the company Ezra was looking for.

While his daughter went from craft table to craft table exploring, Ezra chatted with one of our nurses:

"So you always have an RN on site?" he asked.

"Yes, I am the RN today," Jay answered. "Trained medical assistants can give shots, but we want to have a senior staff on each mobile team to handle complex questions, as well as manage a severe reaction, such as if someone needs a shot of epinephrine."

"Could your team set up to give an IV infusion instead? I am trying to make it easier to get these monoclonal antibody treatments out for people." Ezra wanted to get a feel for what our company could do, and how fast we could do it. He was impressed with the way we had transitioned from mass vaccinations to mobile teams. And today he was impressed with the connection with the Spanish-speaking community. I am not sure if they told him that the first time we showed up at Yard Birds, we were chased away by fearful and angry shopkeepers. But the team had made such a connection with the community that we were now welcomed.

Soon, Patrick was driving to the Department of Health warehouse with Jennifer Jewitt, whom we usually called "JJ" to distinguish her from the many other Jennifers we had working, including my wife. Neither was sure what this was about—the message they had heard

---

[1] Owen Sexton, "'I'm just happy to be done with it': Yard Birds property sold to 'investor,' longtime owner says," *The Chronicle*, July 8, 2024, https://www.chronline.com/stories/im-just-happy-to-be-done-with-it-yard-birds-property-sold-to-investor-longtime,345572.

from Mr. Stark was a little cryptic.

At the far end of the warehouse, Patrick and JJ passed very full refrigerators. They found Ezra behind one of these fridges, a notebook in one hand and a screwdriver in the other, a huge smile on his face, ready to talk.

"What are all these refrigerators full of?" asked Patrick, after introductions were over. "I thought you didn't store COVID shots here."

"Oh, those aren't vaccines," replied Ezra, "they're monoclonal antibodies."

JJ piped up: "Why are you storing those? Do you have a treatment center here?"

"No, we don't," answered Ezra patiently. "We keep them here and distribute out as needed to the clinical sites that are administering them." Ezra looked off into the distance as he contemplated. "September 16, 2021: that was the day my life changed," he said wistfully. "My job description talked a lot about preparing medical countermeasures. But that day the feds shifted responsibility for these meds to the states, and I have been in charge of them ever since."

Ezra seemed to come back to the present with a rush of energy. "Well, welcome to the warehouse," he said as he wiped his oily hands. "If you could store some of these monoclonals, I wouldn't have to babysit fridges and I could focus more on saving lives."

"We for sure can help you with that," said Patrick. "We are about to have more warehouse space than we can use, and plenty of people trained on keeping medications cool."

Ezra sat Patrick and JJ down in his office and for the next hour and a half gave a highly informed account of the challenges of distributing the monoclonal antibodies. He explained that more politically conservative states generally had easier access to IV antibody therapies, possibly because people considered them safer and more natural than the COVID vaccines. State governments and local providers adapted to (or possibly encouraged) this sentiment and set up locations where the antibodies could be given. The most monoclonals were given in the southern states and the fewest on the West Coast.[1]

The monoclonals were formulations of certain antibodies copied from people who had already recovered from COVID-19. The FDA gave emergency authorization to the first anti-COVID monoclonals early in November of 2020,[2] a month before the first US vaccines came out. They were typically given by infusion into the veins, though some were given by intramuscular injection. Except for convalescent plasma,[3,4] the monoclonals were the only therapies at the time that were shown to have some effectiveness in early COVID infections, before someone was sick enough to be in the hospital.

The health department had been getting complaints that there were not enough locations in Washington State where people could get monoclonal antibody treatments. As the de facto coordinator for these therapies, Ezra was trying his best to make them available, especially to the smaller communities.

Ezra was a superhero force in this fight, with endless energy, connections, and ideas. He seemed to know every pharmacist in the state, contacted everyone giving antibodies, and had an uncanny knowledge of the latest medical information on COVID. Soon Patrick had us working under Ezra's direction, and we helped supply nurses to

---

[1] Timothy Anderson, "Uptake of Outpatient Monoclonal Antibody Treatments for COVID-19 in the United States: a Cross-Sectional Analysis," *Journal of General Internal Medicine* 36, no. 12 (2021): 3922–3924, https://doi.org/10.1007/s11606-021-07109-5.

[2] Daniele Focosi et al., "Monoclonal antibody therapies against SARS-CoV-2," *Lancet Infectious Disease* 22, no. 11 (2022): e311–e326, https://doi.org/10.1016/S1473-3099(22)00311-5.

[3] Convalescent plasma is plasma donated by someone who has recently recovered from an infection such as COVID. Theoretically at least, this would be ideal to treat someone early in COVID, because antibodies to a current strain would be present, as well as other factors that maybe we are not yet good at measuring. It had mixed evidence in studies on COVID patients but perhaps was not studied as thoroughly in early cases. And perhaps it did not get more attention because it is not a "drug" that can be patented and become a source of income for the pharmaceutical industry.

[4] Quigly Dragotakes et. al., "Estimates of actual and potential lives saved in the United States from the use of COVID-19 convalescent plasma," *PNAS* 121, no. 41 (2024), https://doi.org/10.1073/pnas.2414957121.

hospitals and clinics that were offering monoclonal antibody treatments to outpatients. We set up our own site in Lewis County to give monoclonals, operating out of Northwest Pediatrics after-hours. JJ's job grew.

Up to this point, we had been doing only prevention. Moving into treatment was a major expansion, and it took a lot of work. We increased our interactions with hospitals and had more nurses working under the direct supervision of others. We also had to deal with the reality that travel nurses in hospitals were being paid a lot of money.[1] How would we pay our nurses in comparison? Who would keep up with the hospital's HR departments? JJ, working from home and on the road, handled these and many more issues one by one. She called, organized, connected, trained, re-called, checked credentials, reassured, and double-checked. In managing so many things at once, JJ's experience as an ICU nurse served her well. It seemed like every morning, Ezra had a new task, a new hospital needed help, and another pharmacy was asking for more doses. Ezra wanted to review what we were doing in close detail. This was fine, but it did take a fair bit of time.

We knew that for these therapies to be effective, they needed to be used early in the infection, before people were sick enough to be in the hospital. This was the stage where more lives could be saved, in the outpatient setting, especially for those who refused vaccination or whose immune systems would not respond well to the vaccine. But these treatments were not for everyone: they were only appropriate for those at the highest risk. Making this judgment of risk was complicated and needed a provider's input. One challenge was that many providers were not yet familiar with the treatments.

I gave some Zoom lectures to help doctors and others get up to speed, but few tuned in to listen. I really didn't want to form our own provider group, but I was beginning to wonder if that was what it was going to take.

---

[1] Jean Lee, "Travel nurses' gold rush is over. Now, some are joining other nurses in leaving the profession altogether," *NBC News*, September 3, 2022, https://www.nbcnews.com/health/health-news/travel-nurses-gold-rush-now-are-joining-nurses-leaving-profession-alto-rcna45363.

In the midst of managing difficult personnel, death threats at the testing site, and long Ezra conferences, Patrick, JJ, Angi, Tessa, and I had a conference call one evening: "We have this situation with the monoclonal antibodies," I said, and we discussed the need for outpatients to take them before they were that sick, and the challenge of identifying which patients needed them.

Patrick pushed us: "We have our own testing sites. Why don't we just refer people from there that are appropriate for treatment?"

"It's not that easy," Tessa said, shy to show her extensive smarts. "You can't send everyone who is positive for COVID. The treatment center will be overwhelmed, and people will be treated when they don't need it."

"What about treating them there at the Greyhound station?" I asked.

Angi stated the obvious: "Dr. Bunge, you know what a run-down place that is. It might be possible, but patients will not feel good about getting an IV in a boarded-up building." I knew it was true, though I wanted to explore all the options. We had talked about painting the inside of the Greyhound, but the heating system was touch and go, ventilation was poor, and yes, it was still boarded up. We were only using the open drive-through area.

JJ spoke up: "We need to refer the appropriate patients to the treatment centers. And we can't wait for the patient's regular doctor to do it, who doesn't know what is happening." She was right, of course. Practical and straightforward.

"Patrick, we need to figure out liability insurance for providers," I said. It was clear from this short conversation that if we wanted to refer people for treatment, we would need to get our own provider pool going. Once again, the regular medical system was stuck and not responding to the COVID need.

I started shopping for additional liability insurance coverage for myself and other clinicians so that we could do telehealth as needed to help coordinate the antibody therapies. I was surprised when the insurance companies were hesitant. They explained they had been burned before by insuring small telehealth companies that wound up being weak in quality. Even after pressure from our large medical system partners, they would not budge. An insurance broker told me that if we did not have an actual physical office in addition to telehealth, they would not cover us at all. They may also have been nervous that we focused on COVID treatments, with unknown risks and so much political heat. This was new territory for the medical field. I had heard that nurses had an organization that helped them get liability insurance, so we asked around and called the Nurses Service Organization (NSO).

In general, nurses and dentists organize more streamlined systems for themselves than doctors do. Or perhaps they simply don't tolerate the same level of nonsense. For example, to get liability insurance, doctors must fill out reams of paperwork detailing what kind of work they do and whether or not they have been sued. The doctor sends in this stack to a broker or directly to one of the larger liability companies and then waits. After a week or more, the broker calls back with a quote that sounds better than it is. The charge goes up after the first year, and the second, and on and on. Even doctors who practice for only one year have to purchase additional "tail" coverage later because they can be sued for years afterward. Brokers give you non-explanations as to why it is so complicated, or, in our case, why they couldn't cover us at all.

In contrast, if a nurse or nurse practitioner wants insurance, they go to the NSO web page. There, they answer some questions and press a button. Their insurance starts immediately. They pay for the year, tail included. No games, no tricks, no dizzy back and forth.

We reimbursed our nurse practitioners to get NSO coverage. I already had medical director coverage for myself and others answering their questions, and we made sure this covered more than just vaccine questions, but this meant only our nurse practitioners could do telehealth. I thought that this would be temporary when we started, and somebody would eventually see logic, or the state would make the insurance companies cover doctors to do telehealth for us, but that never happened. Since we could only cover nurse practitioners, we hired three of them part time. They did a superb job on the phone and the video calls we set up.

Another monoclonal antibody formulation, Evusheld, was developed for high-risk individuals with a weak immune system due to cancer or other reasons, or who couldn't take the vaccine or may have a poor response to it. This formulation was an altered form of antibodies that stayed in the body for months and helped prevent COVID. The one tricky thing about it was the way it was given: two shots the same day, one in each buttock, every six months. We worked with several health system partners to set up clinics for this, mostly focusing on cancer patients taking chemotherapy. JJ took this over as well, with Tessa assisting her.

We had outgrown our office. We had more refrigerators for vaccines and now other therapies, a growing mountain of supplies for mobile clinics, and more people working on administrative tasks. Finding a place with both good office space and easy-to-access warehouse space was tricky. We wound up moving into a building just next to the complex we were already in. Patrick thought we would never use such a big facility, but we soon outgrew it too, and had to rent even more of the same building a few months later. We were saving more lives, although with the therapies, it took more resources—money, time, and medical effort—for each life saved.[1]

If only more people would take the vaccine!

---

[1] The information is somewhat limited, but this study confirms that the expense per life saved using the monoclonal antibodies is very high: Stephanie Popping et al., "Health Outcomes and Cost-effectiveness of Monoclonal SARS-CoV-2 Antibodies as Pre-exposure Prophylaxis," *Jama Network Open* 6, no. 7 (2023): https://doi.org/10.1001/jamanetworkopen.2023.21985.

Chapter Twenty-Two: Everything at Once

[God] has filled them with skill to do all kinds of work...
– Exodus 35:35 (NIV)

There are no specialists, only vested interests.
– Walther Rathenau[1]

E verything happened at once at the end of 2021. COVID death numbers shot up, we started with treatments and telehealth, Paxlovid was approved for emergency use, and Bird's Eye Medical sent people to Kenya, moved into a bigger office locally, and opened another office across the state. And, I got sick.

Who thought when it started in 2019 that the world would still be battling COVID two years later? If you sign up for the sprint, and you realize after you start that it is a marathon, what are you supposed to do? I suppose it's a lot like many things in life. On the one hand, you are disappointed that the problem is not solved, the relationship is not perfect, the project took so much more time than you thought it would. But on the other hand, you are thankful you didn't know at the beginning how hard it was going to be or how long it was going to take, because you would have been scared off. Maybe you would have never

---

[1] John Lukacs, *Confessions of an Original Sinner* (Ticknor and Fields, 1990), 272. (Note that Walther Rathenau may not be the original source of this quote.)

started school, gotten married, had a child, opened that restaurant, or even gotten out of bed.

The death rates across the country were up in mid-September 2021, and then down again in mid-November. Did we open our testing site just in time for nothing? I would have been OK with that—better safe than sorry. But "down" still meant 1,000 people per week were dying, so I encouraged the staff to carry on.

"We got a call from another county," Patrick said one day. I was having trouble keeping track of all the counties we had contracts with by this point. Besides which we had people working in most of the counties anyway with the state contract as well for mobile teams. At least I was learning more about my state. But I only half paid attention to Patrick as he spoke. Payroll nights took so long already. I should ignore him, I thought. I waited for my hospice computer to warm up, but the system was too slow, so it was hard to pretend I was busy. He continued: "It's San Juan County."

That piqued my interest. The San Juans are a delightful group of islands between Washington's Northwest Coast and Canada's Vancouver Island. They are a relaxing vacation spot, lush with rolling hills and lavender fields, with resorts and boat moorage included for leisure sailors. According to the plaques at former army camps on the main island, the US and Canada both had soldiers stationed there at opposite ends of the island, as both countries claimed the San Juans. They were once close to fighting over the islands after a dispute about a pig in the 1850s, but cooler heads prevailed at the last minute. Later, Kaiser Wilhelm I of Germany arbitrated the case and the US wound up with the islands.[1]

Patrick continued: "The county says they don't have many pharmacies or doctors' offices on the islands, so they asked the National Guard for help with their first COVID shots. But now their population of mostly retired people who live there year-round is asking for the next iteration of the vaccines. They want to partner with Bird's Eye."

---

[1] Confirmed by: "San Juan Islands," *Wikipedia, The Free Encyclopedia*, last modified December 20, 2024, https://en.wikipedia.org/w/index.php?title=San_Juan_Islands&oldid=1264055788.

"Hm," I said as the gears turned. I knew Patrick could get this contract going with no problem. We had the setup, the nurses, and the mobile ability. Jennifer would add the county to her binders to track the checks. Marshall was a master of logistics coordination, ensuring all the gear was available and functioning. Roberta had a team of schedulers working under her now. But I had something else on my mind that Patrick and I had talked about previously: "I am not against going to the San Juan Islands—I love the San Juans! But I don't want to just help the well-to-do. I know it's easier to help those who don't really need that much help. But what about those who without us will not get any attention? We need to prioritize those who truly need us, though it may be harder."

Patrick knew what I was talking about. We were again at work in Lewis County with some testing and had successful mobile vaccine clinics there through our connections, such as with Latino community groups. But we also knew of more need in Benton and Franklin Counties on the east side of the mountains. And we even had talked about other nations as well, especially with the lack of access to high-quality vaccines in sub-Saharan Africa. Patrick and I agreed: We would help San Juan County, but we would also open an office in Franklin County, to store vaccines and to be open to other work in that area. It made little business sense—we had no contract with either Benton or Franklin—but that was where the need was greatest, and that was where we were going to go.

"Thank you, Patrick, for working with me on this," I said once we had agreed and he was preparing an email back to the San Juan County contact, "but my neck is hurting and I need to go home and lie down." *The stress must be getting to me*, I thought. Good thing we kept the home office set up in Nathan's old bedroom. I went home to alternate between bed and my adjustable desk. I used this strategy more and more as my neck pain worsened.

Soon we opened an office across the mountains in the town of Pasco, and we took turns visiting there and helping get it up to speed. Pasco, Richland, and Kennewick make up the Tri-Cities, near where the Snake River enters the Columbia. My wife and I enjoyed the river walk in Richland as well as the variety of food in the area. Our favorite was a hole-in-the-wall restaurant near our office in Pasco where we had to point at pictures to get our food since we don't know Spanish. We formed a fantastic small staff who managed vaccines, arranged clinics, and ran monoclonal antibody treatments next to the Hispanic Chamber of Commerce. Being there was so useful to help build relationships with local healthcare providers, community groups such as Spanish-speaking farm workers, and others. Community buy-in is key to public health.

The first San Juan Island vaccine clinic trip was a great success. We had no problem getting nurses to sign up to go to the islands, even though it was November and not the most pleasant time of year for it. The residents there were highly motivated, organized, and ready for their shots. They gathered in the community center and got jabbed while a folk band played. The team went to centers on all three islands, and the county health department was a joy to work with. It was a cohesive community with a singular focus: fight COVID. The islands were a model of how public health should work in America.

In the meantime, I visited my own primary care doctor's office. "How's the COVID work going?" he asked me.

"Good, but so busy," I replied. "I know I am stressed, but I've been having trouble walking around the block, where usually I run several miles at a time. And I get this cramping neck pain on the left side." My doctor knew how much stress I was under and how much I was working, and that was what he focused on. We talked more about my symptoms, including that I had needed a urinary catheter for a couple of weeks. "Maybe I should get an MRI?" I asked him. "Maybe I have a slipped disc there. Sometimes when I look down, I get a shooting pain down my leg."

"Your neurological exam is completely normal at this point, so it is unlikely anything will show up on MRI. A slipped disc in the lumbar spine would be more likely to cause urinary symptoms," he said, which I agreed with. It is hard to doctor the doctor. "But I'll order a scan of the neck anyway."

He ordered the MRI, but insurance took its time to approve it. I resisted the urge to go to the ER, the only place I could get an MRI quickly. In the meantime, I waited for the meandering process of insurance. I wasn't getting worse, anyway.

Around this time, Patrick and I realized we needed more help in leadership. By now we had so many projects going at once. We were talking about this one evening on yet another Zoom call:

"We could try to hire leaders, but our setup is quite unique, and it will take them some time to even get used to what is going on," I said. "Plus, we probably need a nurse leader—I can tell our nursing staff would be more comfortable if they knew there was an RN at a higher level in the company."

"If we designate leaders from our existing staff, that will speed up making a team," Patrick reflected, "but we will wind up with people without as much leadership background."

"If we do that, we will need to focus on training them in leadership principles. And we have to make a team out of them," I reasoned. We prayed about it and started talking about who to pick. We grouped our projects into three divisions and looked internally for leaders.

It didn't take us long to form the team. Marshall Bishop was the ever-working, ever-capable former restaurant manager whom I had hired for logistics. We put him in charge of the office, with Sarah to help, and kept him in charge of the mobile teams overall. Marshall's strength in managing details had the resulting challenge of allowing others to own the mobile teams under him.

Long we tasked with taking over our medical supply, storage, and distribution, as by this time he was the head of the vaccine managers. He had the same detail focus as Marshall, and the same challenge of strengthening those under him in their own leadership. Long was so committed to the cause that it was difficult for those under him to keep up.

JJ took her time deciding whether she wanted to join the leadership team. She wanted to be sure this was the right fit for her and that she understood what we expected. But once she came on board, she was completely committed. Her strength was that she saw the people under her as her responsibility and she nurtured and protected them, not focusing only on the projects themselves. The associated challenge for her was seeing and supporting other people besides her own team.

We met regularly as a leadership team. We read leadership books together and talked about them weekly, including Good to Great,[1] The Five Dysfunctions of a Team,[2] and Start with Why.[3] I challenged people to continue their formal education as well.

JJ and Marshall: capable, well meaning, hard working, both of them. They had their worst scrap alone in the conference room, waiting for the new leadership group's first meeting together.

"The meeting hasn't even started yet, and are you criticizing me so sharply? We are supposed to be a team," JJ said, defending herself from Marshall's attack.

"If your people would do their job, I wouldn't have to do it for them," Marshall raised his voice a bit, throwing gasoline on the fire.

"Their names are Holly and Wendy, they are not nameless 'people.' They are highly qualified nurses who can't give vaccines without needles. Do you expect them to buy used needles on the street or something?"

Patrick, Long, and I walked in cheerily. We hadn't heard them. We cluelessly stopped the war of words before things got even worse, though we wondered why they were silent for a while.

To their immense credit, Marshall and JJ both made the leadership team work. They did amazing jobs in their sections, despite the sword and shield they each kept at the ready for various battles between each other over the months to come. I remained ignorant of these as I imagined my team a finely flavored stew of trust and mutual respect.

Would the group we made rise to the challenges to come? We didn't know what next thing would come our way, and it depended on what COVID would do. But we had a leadership team. How useful and fruitful that team would be over the next year.

[1] Jim Collins, *Good to Great* (Random House Business Books, 2001).
[2] Patrick Lencioni, *The Five Dysfunctions of a Team: A Leadership Fable* (Jossey-Bass, 2002).
[3] Simon Sinek, *Start with Why: How Great Leaders Inspire Everyone to Take Action* (Penguin, 2011).

Chapter Twenty-Three: Pills for Life

In everything, therefore, treat people the same way you want them to treat you…

— Matthew 7:12a (NASB)

It is ironic, but not accidental, that medicine's great technical power should arrive in tandem with great confusion about the standards and goals for guiding its use.

— Leon Kass[1]

J J had nurses working at several sites in the state, including in Spokane, though it was a real challenge to keep track of staff without a manager there locally. People are not simply computers you can hook up to a long-distance cable. But we did help expand the provision of the monoclonal antibodies in Spokane, which is the medical referral center for a large area of the state, as well as part of Idaho.

When Paxlovid[2] received emergency approval in December of 2021, I thought that this easy-to-take and very effective pill to reduce COVID severity and deaths would quickly be prescribed to high-risk people by their regular providers. But that did not happen nearly as

---

[1] Leon Kass, "Regarding the End of Medicine and Pursuit of Health," *The Public Interest* 40 (1975): 11–42.

[2] Paxlovid is the brand name. This is a pill made of two antiviral drugs with generic names Nirmatrelvir and Ritonavir.

much as it should have, probably for several reasons. In part, drug company Pfizer did not use its usual rollout process with education focusing on clinicians and general advertising for the population at large. Why spend money on advertising when the government is paying for it anyway? The emergency use category probably limited this as well. Paxlovid also has significant interactions with many other medications, which takes some training for the provider to understand before they use it. So, the pills sat in hospitals unused while people were dying. We quickly expanded our telehealth capabilities to incorporate this and the other new pill, Molnupiravir. Not only were we able to advise our COVID-positive patients from the test site to discuss this with their doctor, but we could also now offer our own nurse practitioner to connect with them on the phone or secure video chat, review their history and medications, and recommend either Paxlovid, Molnupiravir, monoclonal antibodies, or supportive care alone. We later called this process test-to-treat, about a week before President Biden announced plans to initiate what he also called test-to-treat in pharmacies across the country, a promise which was very difficult for him to keep.[1]

After our nurse practitioners added Paxlovid to our telehealth options, Ezra, our state contact for monoclonal antibodies, visited to meet with Patrick and JJ. He was happy with our new office, which besides other functions, had enough room to store many thousands of doses of monoclonal vaccines in our multiplying supply of medical fridges.

"How is your work with the new treatments going?" asked Ezra.

"Great!" replied JJ, "but we have been as busy as bees between the testing, Evusheld clinics, supporting Spokane and the other centers, and now getting much busier with our telehealth."

Ezra nodded sympathetically. We were doing this telehealth Paxlovid work pro bono for now, considering how to bill for it through insurance, but Ezra knew about it. "I just got out of a meeting this morning with my main medical boss, Dr. Lutz, and others." This was the

---

[1] Hannah Recht, "How the Test to Treat Pillar of the US Covid Strategy Is Failing Patients," *KFF Health News*, April 15, 2022, https://kffhealthnews.org/news/article/test-to-treat-biden-covid-failing-patients-pharmacies-cvs/.

same Dr. Lutz who was fired in Spokane, now working for the state. "They wanted me to ask you if you could expand to offer these same services to the entire state. Dr. Lutz says that most pharmacies won't be able to easily offer 'test-to-treat,' at least not right away. We have supplies of Paxlovid and Molnupiravir, but we do not have a way to get them to the people."

Patrick and JJ looked at each other. Finally, JJ blurted out, "That's just how we roll." We were almost getting used to the crazy new assignments, the impossible goals, the ridiculous expansions. "I will have to run it by Dr. Bunge," Patrick said, "but there should be no problem."

That night on a group Zoom call, Patrick and JJ told me about the ask. I had spent the day seeing hospice patients in their homes, including a pediatric patient born with a severe genetic disorder, a woman with a painful tumor who had been in bed for years despite her active mind, and one man who was committed to taking his own life out of fear of what pain might come with his cancer. Most of the time, hospice work is not that technically challenging for the doctor, but it comes with a heavy dose of emotional swings and moral quandaries. You need all the resilience you can muster when caring for the dying. Was it odd that I alternated between trying to save lives and attending to those at the end of life?

"How many people per day are we talking about?" I asked after they explained the need for telehealth to me. I knew there was a need, but the last thing I expected was that someone would want us to expand from our two testing sites to the whole state.

"We don't really know," JJ explained. "But they want us to be able to see several hundred patients per day."

Patrick had a spreadsheet of course. It was mostly made by Tessa, who estimated how many people we would need in various roles: administrators, nurses, and others. Patrick briefly reviewed it with us. I started thinking about how I was going to recruit more nurse practitioners. Others could help, but as the doctor, I would need to be the primary one to recruit and interview these clinicians. And I was so tired, fatigued from the pain in my neck and my generalized weakness, limited in walking. I wondered: could I do this job?

"Tell the state yes," I said quietly, "but also tell them we don't need to be the exclusive providers." They were also considering another company that had already started a similar program in another state. I wasn't sure we could meet the whole need by ourselves, so if someone else could help, so much the better. "Also, Patrick," I added, "rent the upstairs." We had rented only the main floor portion of the suite in the building we were in, and the upstairs was still empty. We would need that space.

Our goal was to hire, as soon as possible, enough nurse practitioners to have five on duty for eight hours every day of the week. I would need to supervise them, review their charting, keep the algorithms up to date, and monitor how these new meds were doing. I guessed we would not actually have enough work to keep all these clinicians busy, but we wanted to be ready if they were needed. I would need to find a few full-time providers and a bunch of per diem,[1] so we could adjust depending on the demand.

I immediately put up job postings on LinkedIn and Indeed. I called friends and asked around on Facebook. The nurse practitioners would need to understand that this project could end at any time. I can only say that God provided. Not only did I get some amazing applications; I met, hired, and worked with a phenomenal crew of individuals, most of whom I have yet to shake hands with since they all worked remotely. Some were out of state, and we had to work out the tax, legal, and licensing issues with them.

While we were growing the team, we were already treating the patients who qualified from our own testing sites. At first, the only pills we could locate were at St. Peter hospital (an illogical place for an outpatient medication to be stored). If we had a patient who needed the treatment, we had to call the hospital to check the supply. Then we would fax an order to St. Peter's and have the patient or their family drive to a certain parking lot at the hospital. They would then call the

---

[1] Per diem, or "as needed" providers. It is not uncommon for hospitals or medical groups to have providers in this status, so that when the workload increases, they ask them to work. Usually, there is no commitment made until those days, weeks, or months of work are agreed upon.

hospital pharmacy for someone to bring the medication out to their car. Somehow, that worked. Soon, regular pharmacies started getting their own supplies, but at first, many pharmacists were nervous about it and had questions for us. It helped to open the physical Paxlovid box, as inside there were clear instructions for the patient, but if you had not yet seen it, it could be difficult for the provider or the pharmacist to explain to the patient how to take the pills.

Paxlovid interacts with a long list of medications. The best resource to help with this was a website put up by the University of Liverpool in the United Kingdom. This web page both flagged the interactions and provided suggestions regarding how to adapt the medications when the interactions were mild.

I was not one of the frontline providers on our team, due to the liability issue, but I had weekly online meetings with the nurse practitioners where we reviewed questions and cases together. They called me with questions daily, especially at first. I regularly communicated with my infectious disease specialist connections when we had questions. We relied heavily on the published recommendations of the Infectious Disease Society of America (IDSA). It turned out to be a good thing that the insurance companies would not cover me, or I would have probably jumped in to see the patients myself and done too much. As it was, I was available to the nurse practitioners to answer their questions and reach out to others when I could not. And I had so much other work to do, which by this time was mostly leadership related, which made me thankful for the leadership classes I had taken at Faith University in Tacoma.

Tessa and JJ quickly expanded our system modeled on a regular clinic: the online patient would first "see" a receptionist, who would schedule them on Solv if they hadn't yet scheduled their own appointment. The MA or nurse collected data that was still missing, such as medication lists, which are so important for the drug interaction issue. Then the patient (still in their chair at home or on their cell phone somewhere) "met" the provider for their appointment. After this visit, if medications were prescribed, the provider sent them electronically to the pharmacy for the patient to pick up, or coordinated an antibody therapy.

At first we used Simple Practice, a rudimentary electronic medical record (EMR) that was built for psychologists. It worked to hold notes, but could not send meds to the pharmacy or easily organize things like problem lists. We needed a real medical EMR. Epic, the industry leader that we used at the hospital, is way too complicated to implement quickly, prohibitively expensive, and only available to large hospitals and huge clinic systems. Before the state tasked us, we had already gone through the process of picking an EMR. I had chosen DocLinks, a very decent program developed by a local cardiologist. I picked it because I knew that they could quickly adapt it to what we were doing and they believed in our project. However, it was a challenge for the staff and providers to use what looked and felt like by now an old program.

Our staff and the DocLinks team worked to get everything up and running, including connecting it to Solv and the University of Washington lab. We were able to use DocLinks to order monoclonal antibodies, track the people and clinics we ran for Evusheld, and then add the telehealth work. As they were getting it all going, many times my team was ready to pull their hair, but once again we did what we had to do to treat the people who asked for help.

Soon our telehealth system was accessible by anyone in the state. Numerous testing sites gave out our number and Solv's web connection for our service. I met regularly with our group of nurse practitioners to review cases and share updates.

The Omicron wave was in full swing, the hospitals were full again, and though many more people had already been vaccinated, plenty still refused. Many of them also avoided getting treatments, thinking they were not that ill, at least not yet. And so they missed the window where these medications are most effective—the early stage of COVID.

"Let's take another step," I told the leaders at our testing site one day. They had already taken so many steps to change things around to see what would work and what wouldn't.

"What else can we do?" Angi said. "We are already screening to catch the high-risk people." We had a short questionnaire for anyone coming to the testing site. If they screened positive for severe COVID risk factors, we offered them a rapid pathway: both a rapid test at no cost and a PCR test. If the rapid test was positive, our nurses called them the same day or early the next day for more detailed questions to see if they should talk to a provider about treatment.

"Can we do a one-stop-shop for them here at the testing site?" I asked. "If they have a positive rapid test, we can give them the medication right there."

"It is going to be so much more complex to store medications here," said the lead MA for the site. She and others did such a great job, I hated to stress them out and stretch them even more. But we wanted to see if it would work. We had those at higher risk wait in their car in the parking lot until the rapid test result was complete (10–15 minutes). If it was positive, the staff would schedule them with a provider by video call right there on their phone or our tablet. We had the two medications available and had the pharmacist come on video call or phone call after the provider was done, to explain to the patient how to take them.

The process did work, and it really was the test-to-treat model that President Biden had envisioned. But we only did this for about a week. Many people were annoyed by having to wait in their cars for the rapid test to finish; they preferred for someone text them with the result. Trying to get people hooked up with telehealth and then the pharmacist out in the open while passing things back and forth through car windows also was difficult and something patients didn't really appreciate. By this time enough pharmacies had the medications that most patients could get them from their own pharmacies. So we went back to our previous system.

And what about Africa? We were doing so much for people who refused vaccines, what about those who had no access to vaccination at all? But our people were stretched so thin already.

Chapter Twenty-Four: Out of Africa

Truly I tell you, whatever you did for one of the least of these brothers and sisters of mine, you did for me.
— Matthew 25:40 (NIV)[1]

It is the mark of an educated man to look for precision in each class of things just so far as the nature of the subject admits.
— Aristotle[2]

P atrick and I were especially concerned about the COVID situation in sub-Saharan Africa. I knew from volunteering over the years that medical systems there, especially in rural areas, have limited resources. And we could tell from the news that the better vaccines (Moderna and Pfizer) were much less available. We contacted large non-governmental organizations (NGOs) we thought would likely be involved, but it was difficult to get information. So many of their usual projects were put on hold by COVID, and American staff had come home. Patrick had a friend with World Vision who could get some time off, and eventually, we decided to send the pair of them on a fact-gathering trip to Kenya to get a better picture of the situation, identify NGOs or agencies involved with vaccine distribution, and see if there was anything we could do to help. If they could use nurses, we were talking about sending those who were

---

[1] Jesus speaking to his disciples.
[2] Aristotle, *Nicomachean Ethics*, https://genius.com/Aristotle-nicomachean-ethics-chap-13-annotated.

willing. Patrick and his friend left for two weeks in January of 2022.

I already had a few connections in Kenya to get him started, but Patrick quickly found many more contacts. They met with health officials, hospital heads, and others during their short trip. They identified two NGOs that appeared to be effectively supporting COVID vaccine efforts in Kenya. One was a branch of the Clinton Foundation, and the other was Amref,[1] an NGO formed in 1957 by surgeons who used small airplanes to help deliver medical care and surgical support to mission hospitals in several African countries.[2] Amref now works in many areas of healthcare development. Once Patrick was back, we sent donations to these two organizations designated to continuing their work with COVID vaccines in Africa.

My neck pains and limited walking were a constant drain. But I got to experience what my patients often complained about over the years: the insurance company again refused to approve an MRI. I tried not to let it bother me too much. If I did have a slipped disc, I knew they often go back in on their own, and seeing it on an MRI does not make it better or worse. And I wasn't worse, so it would be best to wait anyway. But that does not mean I had no frustration or anger. I just tried to temper it, keep on with life, and wait.

While we were doing our small project in Africa, Africa was busy changing the world. The world would not understand for months how dramatic a change the new variant, named Omicron, would be. Greek letters are still used by the World Health Organization (WHO) to label the COVID variants it considers most likely to cause a significant threat to health, which they judge "variants of concern."[3,4] They had to skip "Xi" because it looked like the premier of China's name. They skipped

[1] Currently called "Amref Health Africa," the organization originally was known as "The Flying Doctors of East Africa," and at one point "African Medical and Research Foundation," which is where "Amref" came from.
[2] "Our History," Amref Health Africa, accessed September 12, 2024, https://amref.org/our-history/.
[3] "Tracking SARS-Cov-2 Variants," *WHO*, accessed September 14, 2024, https://www.who.int/activities/tracking-SARS-CoV-2-variants/.
[4] "SARS-CoV-2 Omicron Variant," *Wikipedia, The Free Encyclopedia*, last modified June 25, 2025, https://en.wikipedia.org/wiki/SARS-CoV-2_Omicron_variant.

"Nu" because it sounded like the English word "new." The variant they labeled "Omicron" was first reported in South Africa and Botswana in early November 2021.

Omicron represented a major shift in the genetics of the virus: a dramatic change that still puzzles those who study the genes of the tiny foe. Jesse Bloom is a viral geneticist at the Fred Hutchison Cancer Center in Seattle. He came to this conclusion: "Omicron really shows us the need for humility in thinking about our ability to understand the processes that are shaping the evolution of viruses like SARS-CoV-2."[1] Omicron's many genetic changes brought fear to scientists all around the world: What are we going to get next? Will it be even worse now? And it was indeed vastly more infectious to humans than prior variants. Rates of COVID infections rose more rapidly than any other wave, first in South Africa, and then the world over. In January of 2022, our testing site had a line of cars backed up several blocks of Olympia's downtown, something I promised nervous city officials would never happen. What was I to do? I had told the county not to close their site too early.

While Omicron was much more infectious, it turned out to be much less lethal as well. If you look at first-time infections for non-vaccinated people in the US, the pre-Omicron COVID strains were about 100 times more lethal than the yearly influenza virus. Omicron was about 10 times more lethal than the flu. Still a very bad disease, but one could argue it is a very different disease from other COVID strains. It might have been useful to have a new name, something other than COVID-19 Variant Omicron, but that did not happen. At this point, the original COVID is for all practical purposes gone from the earth, replaced by Omicron and its children. I find it so ironic that God used Africa, which received a minuscule fraction of the world's designated COVID-fighting resources, to deliver the world from the original strains of COVID.

Since Omicron was so contagious, it infected close to everyone in the United States. Vaccinated people still had an easier time of it than non-vaccinated, but the sheer numbers all at once including those who

---

[1] Quoted in: Sriti Mallapaty, "The Hunt for the Origins of Omicron," *Nature* 602, no. 7895 (2022): 26–28. (SARS-CoV-2 is another scientific name for COVID-19.)

had never been vaccinated and never had any kind of COVID before meant that even with this less lethal strain, it was a major wave for the country that brought many hospitalizations and deaths. For those who survived, this was a type of vaccine for those who had refused the vaccine. The deaths showed how many people had immune systems that previously had not seen the virus at all—either by infection or vaccine.

Nobody could see this clearly while we were going through it. All we knew then was that people were sick and dying. Hospitals filled up, though in much less proportion to the number of positive tests. Our telehealth team was overwhelmed initially, but we caught up and were able to offer treatment medications to all those high-risk people who wanted them.

One thing became difficult to discern as time went on: who really was benefiting from the early treatments we were offering? It was becoming more and more obvious that Omicron wasn't as dangerous as prior strains, but still, you could get sick and even die. We still did not know the exact risks. We had people who had received multiple COVID vaccinations by this time, were young and healthy, had minor symptoms from their current COVID infection, and called our provider line, insisting on Paxlovid. Our providers were challenged to find the right way to answer these requests.

"JJ and Tessa, I need to talk to you," said Tim, one of our hardworking young men. Tim had worked for months at the testing site and was pulled to the office to help with the monoclonal antibody project and other work. He was obviously stressed. The two nurses let him into their office and closed the door. His face was strained, his lips were drawn tight. Did he have marital issues? Was he sick? He usually was so animated and talkative, but today he was silent as his eyes darted nervously about the room. They were all standing in silence, and Tessa and JJ weren't quite sure what to do next.

Tim focused on the whiteboard on the far wall. The nurses had picked this room to maximize their whiteboard space, as they talked and drew out the plans for the many projects that were going on. Tim erased the board and wrote his name in the center with a circle around it. He then started listing the things he was doing. He started with "answer the phone," and added things under that, phone related. He then wrote

"Evusheld," since he was coordinating many of the Evusheld clinics, and listed what it took to make sure those were all running well. He listed, and listed, and listed, with lines going here and there, the many projects and details he had to worry about. Tessa and JJ tried to hold it in out of respect for this man who was working so hard, but they couldn't help but giggle. By the time he was done, the board was filled with Tim the Octopus, his eight legs stretching out to the various activities.

JJ immediately started to assign some of Tim's tasks to others and worked with him more to understand what we needed to do to keep the important work going without burning him and others out. When you are changing so fast, and people believe in what they are doing, it is easy to lose sight of the fact that everyone has limits.

One difficult area was facilities with outbreaks. We had monoclonal antibodies, and later, the oral medications. Should we go in and give treatments to everyone in a nursing home if they called us? They were high risk, so probably all would qualify for treatment. On the other hand, so many of them had been vaccinated. We felt these were not completely benign treatments and that there should be a discussion with each patient, or with the family if the patient was unable to discuss options. What if the patient was on hospice status and didn't want aggressive treatments? This was not something like the vaccines, where the facility staff could ask the patient and family in advance, there was a general understanding of how vaccines work, a nurse could lead the risk discussion, the person was not sick at the time, and our team could vaccinate all those who wanted it. The treatment question was much more nuanced and needed more of a clinician–patient relationship. The few facility outbreaks that the state asked us to respond to were difficult for this reason. Perhaps another doctor would have fewer qualms about blanketing a group of people with medications, but I had the qualms and thus the challenge.

We thought about expanding our test-to-treat and telehealth capabilities to other states as the months went by. By this time, however, COVID numbers were coming down, the usual system of medical care was starting to pick up with the newer treatments, and the monoclonal antibodies were becoming less useful as more subvariants of Omicron were resistant to them. In addition, Jennifer and I were talking about how much strain the work was having on our relationship. Perhaps this was not the greatest time to expand the company even more. So I said, "No, let's stick just to Washington State." It was the first of many "no's." Each one was painful for me, as I knew we could do more, and we had such a great team working together. Two things kept me saying "no" more and more as 2022 moved on: my marriage and the way COVID seemed to be behaving, which later we knew had so much to do with how Omicron changed the pandemic.

"Dad, I need to tell you something," my oldest son, David, said to me one day. He was back at work in person, though he switched accounting firms because most of the people at his original company still worked remotely. He realized, as many did, that complete remote work was just too hard on his psyche. David continued: "You and Mom are not getting along that well with the company and all."

"Thanks for your concern," I replied, glad that he felt like he could share with me, but offended that this single guy thought he could teach me about my marriage. "We are doing better, now that the company is more stable, and we are slowing down some. We are even planning to join my sister and help get your grandmother to Hawaii for a couple of weeks, which she will love so much." I heard David in part, but the other part was my denial. I wanted to keep the company going, and I thought Jennifer and I could do that as long as we sought balance. Besides, didn't he know we were saving lives? What if the virus changed again, and we had to expand? And what other public health challenges could we help with?

What was David observing? Jennifer and I were still talking and doing things together, we were still connected. But David said we were not treating each other well like we used to.

"David," I said to him later. "Your mother has issues." And I listed what I considered a summary account of her weaknesses. I thought he would understand, see how patient I had been, commiserate with me over what I had to put up with, and even be proud of me for over 30 years of marriage thus far. Besides, I was the leader of the company. She was only doing the finance, and some others at the company were annoyed with her approach. She could quit at any time.

"Dad, you are not treating her well. She picks on you, but you pick on her, too." Yikes, why was he taking her side? "I remember when you two might have a fight once or twice a year growing up, but it seems like you have that kind of fight every week, or maybe every day." Another blow to my marriage-success ego.

Work distracted me from this question as I buzzed along. Someone once said that a wife is a walking marriage manual, and it is up to the husband to bother to read it. I was OK leaving the manual closed for now. Hadn't 30 years of working at it been enough? Looking back, I am amazed my wife had such patience with the attitude I had. Denial can cause damage, in a marriage as well as on a national scale.

In the meantime, we were hearing about a growing virus threat in Africa: monkeypox (the name was later changed to mpox). What would happen with that, and would we be a part of any response? And we still had our hands full with the testing site, the telehealth work with COVID treatments, our office in Pasco, and mobile vaccination projects.

Chapter Twenty-Five:
Private Public Health

The leprous person who has the disease shall wear torn clothes and let the hair of his head hang loose, and he shall cover his upper lip and cry out, "Unclean, unclean." He shall remain unclean as long as he has the disease. He is unclean. He shall live alone. His dwelling shall be outside the camp.

— Leviticus 13:45–46 (ESV)

Do whatever is right in front of us.

— Dietrich Bonhoeffer[1]

In the beginning, our company had no credibility with local public health, and they shooed us away. But later, the counties and the state came to see our work as essential. By the end of 2021, we were known to several county health departments and the state as a company that could get things done fast. It was not only with the COVID response, but work with mpox and syphilis during 2021 and 2022 also illustrated our abilities and the usefulness of partnership.

When I first heard that mpox (formerly known as monkeypox) was spreading in gay men in the spring of 2022, Patrick and I talked about

---

[1] Dietrich Bonhoeffer, *Ethics* (Fortress Press: 2009), 295.

it. We knew we should keep a close eye on this outbreak and be ready to act as needed and as appropriate. It seemed likely that if it transmitted primarily through same-sex contact in gay men, then it would be easier to control than if it also jumped into the general population. Fortunately, there was already an effective vaccine: the smallpox vaccine. However, the smallpox vaccine has a fair number of side effects. During my time in the military, they gave out the smallpox vaccine, thinking that Iraq's Saddam Hussein might weaponize smallpox (as it turned out, he did not have that capability[1]). Some young men developed inflammation of the heart and its lining as a major side effect.[2] I was not excited to have to give this vaccine too broadly if it was not going to be needed outside the specific group mpox was spreading in currently.

Mpox did not broadly jump to other groups—I only heard of one infection in a child in daycare at the time. But we were ready to help out, and we had one highly motivated nurse spearhead this project. He helped train the other nurses in the vaccine administration, and we staffed several mpox clinics in western Washington. The interventions of public education and the smallpox vaccine were effective, and mpox was relatively short-lived as a significant US outbreak, at least for that round.

Our brief work with syphilis was interesting and instructive, in terms of both our ability to help and respond quickly as well as illustrating some of the challenges of public health.

People without housing living in tent camps were more numerous in our area during and after the COVID pandemic. All the West Coast states faced this dilemma. Part of Washington State's response to COVID was to scale back what the police and others usually did in

---

[1] "No Evidence Iraq Had Smallpox," *CBS News*, September 21, 2003, https://www.cbsnews.com/news/no-evidence-iraq-had-smallpox/.
[2] Renata Engler et. al., "Myocarditis and pericarditis recovery following smallpox vaccine 2002–2016: A comparative observational cohort study in the military health system," *PLoS One* 18, no. 5 (2023), https://doi.org/10.1371/journal.pone.0283988.

limiting and clearing homeless camps,[1] in part because of the knowledge that COVID spread more rapidly in homeless shelters. This meant that many more camps popped up, and some grew considerably. One homeless camp in Olympia was called "the jungle." Adjacent to both a marijuana shop and St. Peter hospital, it was a nightmare place, where mud and filth and drugs mixed.[2] We saw a variety of patients from the jungle regularly at St Peter's: mentally ill, drug users, the violent, the angry disabled, codependent helpers, prostitutes. The list seemed endless. A roadway runs from this area around to the back parking area of St. Peter's. During COVID, people started parking old RVs along this road. Pretty soon, the whole stretch was full and it seemed there was nothing the hospital or the city could do about it. I remember going to work on the COVID wards early in the morning, worrying about my COVID patients, but also concerned about the safety of people wandering the road as we drove in. It wasn't until the end of 2021 that the city started meaningfully working to move the derelict RVs.[3]

"Len called us to see if we could help with a syphilis outbreak," Patrick said one day as I walked down the hall at the office.

"You're kidding, right?" I said, slowing my step as I processed this. "You have to be joking—syphilis is effectively treated by penicillin, and it's now quite rare." I could count on one hand the number of cases I had even heard of in my career, much less an "outbreak."

"Well, Len from Hills and Valleys County[4] says they have an outbreak and wonders if we can help them," Patrick repeated. "It sounds

[1] Natalie Argerious, "Inslee Pushes Legislation Prioritizing Homeless Encampment Removal Near Highways," *The Urbanist*, February 10, 2022, https://www.theurbanist.org/2022/02/10/inslee-pushes-legislation-prioritizing-homeless-encampment-removal-near-highways/.

[2] Austin Jenkins, "Murder Reveals 'Lord of the Flies' Street Culture in Washington's Capital," *NW News Network*, October 14, 2023, https://www.nwnewsnetwork.org/crime-law-and-justice/2013-10-14/murder-reveals-lord-of-the-flies-street-culture-in-washingtons-capital.

[3] Brandon Block, "City Begins Sweeping RV Residents off Ensign Road," *The Olympian*, December 17, 2021, p. A1.

[4] Not the actual county.

interesting, we need to branch out beyond COVID, and it is still public health related.

"The county's hospitals have had an uptick in babies born with syphilis," Patrick explained. "Those babies are in very bad shape. They have been tracking this for a couple of years, and the reality is, women in homeless camps have been prostituting themselves for drugs, contracting syphilis, and getting pregnant. They want our doctor—you—to sign off on treatments for syphilis at a homeless camp their public health nurses have been visiting. They have been testing people there, but they usually guide patients into the clinic when they need therapy. These people don't show up in the clinic. They want to offer treatments on-site."

"What about their own public health doctor? Can't he or she sign off on that?" I asked.

"Well," Patrick paused, "that person refuses." We both laughed.

"We've heard that one before," I said.

"What do you want to do?" asked Patrick. He knew what he wanted me to do, but he allowed me space. Patrick is the only person I know who can combine that calm flexibility so well with a clear goal. Most people in high-stress situations either give way to their own emotions or give up on achieving what they want. There is no way we could have achieved so much as a company without Patrick Hastings and his unique ability to hold these two in tension constantly and nearly flawlessly.

"Give me some time to work on this," I said. "In the meantime, find out what their protocols are and what exactly they expect."

I did some reading. Local hospitals around the country had been reporting an increase in cases of congenital syphilis.[1] This bacterial disease occurs when a pregnant mother's syphilis infection crosses over the placenta to infect the baby. Untreated, about 40% of kids die before birth. Those who survive can develop a myriad of issues, including

---

[1] Centers for Disease Control and Prevention (CDC), "US Syphilis Cases in Newborns Continue to Increase: A 10-Times Increase Over a Decade," *CDC News Release*, November 7, 2023, https://www.cdc.gov/media/releases/2023/s1107-newborn-syphilis.html.

brain damage, bone deformities, and hearing loss. Treatment is complicated and can take a long time.

The more I read, the more I realized how complex syphilis treatment protocols would be, whether we adapted an existing one or wrote our own. It would involve correct interpretation of tests and categorizing people into primary, secondary, and tertiary syphilis. After looking into options, I agreed that it was too complicated for the public health nurses to do by themselves. So I suggested another approach, and the county agreed. One of our highly capable nurse practitioners agreed to go with the public health team and be on site to make treatment decisions and start medications. After training and updates on syphilis, she was ready to go.

This approach did allow treatment on site at the homeless camp. However, even with this intervention, it did not improve the situation very much. Treating syphilis in pregnant women, following up on labs, and checking on progress requires seeing patients more than once or twice, and the camp's residents were simply too transient for that to work well.

Though syphilis is a completely treatable and preventable disease that was mostly eliminated from the US for many years, our nation now has a serious syphilis problem. I cannot see a way to make much headway with syphilis in homeless camps without adding some "teeth" to the effort. By adding "teeth," I mean some freedoms must be curtailed. These women could have been treated, and their kids and the kids of others could have been saved, but the women would need to be placed in a more restricted and structured living environment, whether they agreed to it or not, to get supervised treatments.

This is the uncomfortable reality of public health work: sometimes, to be effective, it requires forcing some people into or away from some behavior. There can be no society without laws, and laws must be enforced to have meaning, whether they are mandatory seatbelt use, restaurant employees washing their hands, airline maintenance schedules, or supervised tuberculosis treatments. Of course, much good public health is done without "enforcement," as creative and motivated public health workers all over the world inform, advertise, explain, and encourage, and then leave the decision to the individual. When possible, that should be the norm, because it limits government overreach and protects individual freedoms.

Yet in every society, there is a balance between freedoms and responsibilities. If a society insists that adults should be allowed to use addictive substances, engage in prostitution to sustain their habit, and refuse treatment for the syphilis or HIV that results, then that society will have to deal with the reality of HIV spread and syphilis babies with brain damage showing up in their hospitals.

This is a very challenging issue, without easy answers. There are and will be disagreements on how to approach the situation. For discussions to occur, much humility is needed as people must listen to each other even though they disagree. Criteria should be debated and discussed, but then decisions must be made. As in many areas, if reasonable people do not deal with the challenging questions and make the difficult decisions, unreasonable people will rise and make those decisions, like them or not.

When we get the balance wrong—either by taking too few precautions or imposing excessive restrictions—people pay with their lives. The very strong public health-focused approach to COVID in mainland China saved millions of lives early in the pandemic. But China's inability to balance this with the changing reality of COVID, especially well after Omicron was the dominant strain, led to a mass revolt of the Chinese people against the draconian system of restrictions and testing. The government then completely lifted the restrictions all at once. The public lacked trust in available vaccines, so people's immune systems were unprepared. There was limited access to treatments such as Paxlovid. This meant many Chinese people died of Omicron. Just how many we may never know. The Chinese experience, as well as our own American failings and high numbers of deaths, illustrates the need for discussion, humility, nuance, patience, humanity, and reason when trying to discern how to strike the best balance between public health and individual liberties.

In the meantime, I was trying to strike my own balance. By late fall of 2022, my marriage was at a crossroads.

Chapter Twenty-Six: The Handoff

So we don't look at the troubles we can see now; rather, we fix our gaze on things that cannot be seen. For the things we see now will soon be gone, but the things we cannot see will last forever.
                                          – II Corinthians 4:18 (NLT)

I always wanted to be somebody, but now I realize I should have been more specific.
                                          – Lily Tomlin[1]

I sat in the basement of St. Peter Hospital in November of 2022. The hospitalist workroom is down in this gloomy, windowless area, but it is well equipped, and my mood picked up once I got past the cement hallways into the actual workroom. I was not assigned any patients that day—I was just catching up on emails and Epic messages—but I still felt a squeeze in my chest, like a rope pulling in opposite directions. The pull one way was my marriage and family, calling out for survival. Pulling the opposite way was the company. I had not told anyone in the company about the decisions Jennifer and I had made—to wrap the project up and be done—so that pull was silent, for now. My struggle that day, that month, that whole last half of 2022, was inside.

---

[1] From the Editors of Portable Press, *Dad Jokes* (Printers Row Publishing Group, 2017), 277.

It was a year already since Jennifer told me that she had had enough. She had said she was willing to keep at it for a few more months, after I explained the COVID situation at the time, with the need for treatments to continue, the large number of unvaccinated Americans, and the like. But as the end of 2022 approached, she insisted that we be done. She was reeling under the stress and wanted our relationship to be better.

To use hospice terminology, I was going through three of the stages of grief: denial, bargaining, and anger. The stages of grief were first described by Elizabeth Kübler-Ross as she and her team interviewed and analyzed terminally ill cancer patients and the evolution of their emotional responses to their diagnosis and progression of disease.[1] Her description, and its adaptations over the years, continue to be very helpful in assisting those who grieve. I knew I was going to lose this company, but I wanted to keep it; thus, I grieved.

I had mostly finished the denial stage. I stayed there for a long time, thinking that Jennifer and I would be fine, that we would weather the storm of the business, that there were no icebergs in the way of the Titanic. In my denial, I had been like others who had been in denial early on during COVID, who had frustrated me so much. I was right there with so many of my patients over the years, who said they did not believe their biopsy report that said "cancer," who swore their cholesterol was better than it was, who only drank "once in a while" while their wife (or husband) shook their head sadly in the corner. I was in denial.

Denial can be a useful coping mechanism, though it can also cause damage. In this case, Jennifer and I were able to do the work we did because we put on hold for a time the energy and love that we needed to give to each other. But now the benefits were decreasing as the damage was increasing. It took special interventions on the part of others to help me see this.

"It's time to give up this company," my friend Dr. Rick Sams had said to me months before. We met on a required Navy rotation during

---

[1] Elizabeth Kübler-Ross, *On Death and Dying* (McMillan, 1969).

medical school and were stationed together several times over our Navy careers. For years we have been close friends. We have been on medical volunteer trips together, sometimes with family members, to Kenya and Haiti. We have the kind of friendship where you can tell each other the hard truth and still talk the next day.

"We are OK," I told Rick at the time. "We pray together and have time to talk about other things, just not that much."

"You are blind," Rick told me on a later phone call. "Listen, mister. What is more important? Your business or your marriage?" Rick knew me and knew that I was stubborn. He loved Jennifer and me, and he knew we had a good marriage. He didn't want to see it lost.

Rick started confronting me soon after the business started, told me to try to keep a balance and not overdo it. By the time I was sitting in the basement of St. Peter's, he had told me several times very clearly on the phone: "Paul, you need to get rid of this company. It doesn't matter how, just get rid of it."

Around the same time Rick was waving his arms and trying to get my attention, and after my son David had already lectured me, the other two kids also sat me down. Erika started, not typically stingy with the drama: "Dad, what is wrong with you? I quit Bird's Eye already. Nathan quit the company. You need to, too."

Nathan, our youngest, is much more tender, but even he chimed in: "Dad, maybe you should consider letting go of the company. I miss you being able to talk to me more."

"Yeah," Erika kept on, "your kids need you, see? Your kids are important, even when they are adults."

I didn't want to give up the company. It was doing good work. And my identity and ego were now tied up with it. But I trusted my kids, and I trusted my friend. I promised them I would quit by the end of the year. That's one way to deal with denial: promise your way out of it. It forces your hand. That is, if you keep your promises.

Anger is another component of the grieving process. During those months, when I wasn't in denial, I was angry. Angry that I had to give up something I had made, that I was in charge of. Anger that I could not continue to work with this fantastic group of people.

Jennifer and I, despite many sparks in the process, agreed that we would try to sell the company. If it did not sell by the end of December, we would simply close it. This is where I moved into bargaining. Even after I had agreed to sell the company, I kept bringing up to Jennifer reasons to keep the company, which was not helpful. Actual bargaining, besides the grief-related internal bargaining, followed as we talked to other companies that had worked during COVID, to see if they were interested in buying, to other business-minded doctors, and to brokers who act as agents in finding interested buyers.

"So, what does your company do besides COVID work?" asked Lance the business broker, as Jennifer and I sat with him and his partner Bill at an upscale restaurant.

"Well, we did some other things, also," and I explained the mpox and the syphilis projects.

"But you are not doing those projects now. Is that correct?" he returned.

"That's right," I said, "but we have a very good system, good people, a great reputation, and the opportunity is there to move into childhood vaccines and other work."

Bill joined in the theme: "It's just that nobody is going to be interested in a company that does COVID work now. People are moving on from COVID and nobody will see the value." These brokers, and others I called, were nice and knowledgeable, and completely not interested.

At the same time, we had a couple of potential buyers from personal contacts—doctors who could see the continued medical value of what we were doing, the relationships we had made, and the capabilities we had. I was confident that one of these doctors would take over the company. But they both called me up and told me for different reasons that no, they were not interested. It wasn't about price; we had not even discussed that yet. But their no was no.

Bargaining. That was what I was doing down in the basement of St. Peter's. I was hanging around wondering if any of these other doctors might be interested. I asked a couple while I was there: were they interested in the business side of medicine? I knew some hospitalists were—they had their hands in private nursing home work or other private endeavors in their off time. But it was again a waste of time, nobody wanted this company.

We were successful in so many areas. We gave out hundreds of thousands of vaccines with quality, compassion, and efficiency. We cared for and honored our employees and built effective and innovative business structures. We started and ran a telehealth clinic and gave out therapies to save even more people from dying from COVID-19. We helped stop mpox. We worked with many partners and kept a large diversity of people working together.

I thought that our company could continue to do many useful things for public health that were not COVID-related. Vaccination rates for regular childhood vaccines had already been lagging and decreased more during COVID.[1] We started the process of getting ready to give childhood vaccines with our mobile teams, making policies and figuring out costs and other things we would need. I put the process on hold, however, because I did not want to start something new if the company might be closing.

I had read several things about selling or closing a company, and the conventional wisdom was to wait as long as possible to tell the employees. Morale goes down, quality can be affected, and people run off to new jobs just when you need them most in the case of a sale. I hated being unable to be completely transparent in meetings with my leadership team. We would talk about issues, and I would make decisions, but the reasons for some of my decisions must have made them wonder.

So here I was, still in the basement, around hardworking, high-quality doctors, unable to find anyone to carry the torch for me. It was then that true sadness and frustration poured in like water filling a barrel, heavier and heavier. The doctors around me were in a different world. Few could even envision owning a company. And even those who would be comfortable owning their own company would still not

---

[1] Ranee Seither et al., "Vaccination Coverage with Selected Vaccines and Exemption Rates Among Children in Kindergarten—United States, 2021–2022 School Year," *Morbidity and Mortality Weekly Report* 72, no. 2 (2023): 26–32, https://doi.org/10.15585/mmwr.mm7202a2.

be interested in a company that focused on public health rather than an individual patient-centered approach.

I tried to delay the announcement that we were closing. At the same time, I wanted to give all of our county and state connections the heads-up so they could adapt, and I wanted to give our employees time to look for new jobs. First, I told Patrick and gave him the impossible offer of keeping the company going on his own, though he would need some way of obtaining enough working capital. He couldn't do that, and a few days later, I announced the closure plan to the leadership team: Marshall, JJ, and Long. They were all so mature and accepting, even though they were frustrated with the decision. They were able to take the information quickly to the rest of the office during that day, and I announced it that evening at our regular company Zoom meeting. My team did not melt or become dysfunctional. They thought of other people, not themselves:

"Hey, Dr. Bunge, we understand," Long said, as the others nodded their heads. They were not angry, they did not dwell on it at all.

"We need to decide who will need to stay around to finish up the work and close up shop," said JJ. She was thinking about her team as well as the needs of the company. The employees would need to know when their last days would be. The team immediately started listing their employees, and we talked about who could do what and who would need to stick around until when. We would honor our contracts, which were through the end of December, and some employees we would ask to stay longer. We had a whole warehouse of supplies to try to liquidate, a van to sell, etc.

Two days later, Marshall came into my office and closed the door. "Dr. Bunge," he said, "there has to be a way to keep the company going."

Marshall is going through his bargaining stage now, I thought. *Don't argue too much. He needs time to process,* I told myself. But what I said out loud was probably too hopeful and reflected my own internal bargaining: "Certainly I will help you the best I can if you can figure out a way to keep the company going," though really by that point, I had no hope for it continuing.

Marshall had the energy, the motivation, and the persistence.

Patrick, Marshall, Jennifer, and I put together a plan that is too creative and complicated to describe well here, something that worked largely because of Patrick's business smarts and Marshall's tenacity. We all prayed over it with the lawyer, which was a unique and wonderful experience in itself, and two years on, Bird's Eye Medical is still doing its work, including many childhood vaccines all over the state, and has expanded outside of Washington as well.

Part of the process was a significant downsizing that we started in earnest even before the end of the year, and then implemented fully in January. We still had to safely disposition much of the supply inventory from the warehouse and the testing site. Tony was able to sell some things. We donated much to Medical Teams International,[1] an organization I had volunteered with in the past.

Jennifer and I still spent several months on paperwork, sorting, and in meetings with Marshall and Patrick, as we had to make scores of decisions in the transition. We were all relatively patient with each other in this process, and we ultimately agreed on the details, which enabled us to complete the transfer.

Though we still were busy, Jennifer and I could see the light at the end of the tunnel by this time, and we could start the process of rebuilding our relationship. So many issues to talk about, each one needing attention that it had not had for the last three years. The work to be done on our marriage was just beginning.

While we were considering the deal with Marshall and Patrick, I said I would still close the company if we couldn't find a medical director for them. Dr. Joel Abbott, amazing friend and doctor that he is, stepped in as medical director for the company and remains so over two years later. I ended up keeping the old Greyhound station where we had our testing site. I would learn a lot about commercial real estate over the next years, but that is another story.

We moved closer to the border with Canada, where we have many relatives, including my mother. I am working more at hospitals again.

---

[1] MTI does a very good job of organizing and vetting supplies that are donated so they are effective when they get overseas.

My mother's memory continues to slowly worsen, and we are going through that journey of ups and downs together.

I learned so much through those three years, but what are the things I need to face now? With my marriage, with others? Who do I need to forgive, and how do I approach that? How do I move on, and how do we as a nation move on?

Chapter Twenty-Seven: Forgive

And whenever you stand praying, forgive, if you have anything against anyone, so that your Father also who is in heaven may forgive you your trespasses.

– Mark 11:25 (ESV)

Forgiving a variety of real-life interpersonal offenses can be effective in promoting different dimensions of mental well-being.

– Sadaf Akhtar and Jane Barlow[1]

I s COVID over? Yes and no. Massive surges overwhelming the hospitals are no more. I still see COVID patients, including sick patients in the ICU, but severe illness caused by COVID is much less common now. We have more advanced treatments for people at various stages. Vaccines still work, especially in the elderly and those with weak immune systems. Though Paxlovid is now heavily promoted at doctors' conferences, its usefulness outside of the severely immunocompromised is much more questionable now. The current strains have become "endemic" rather than "pandemic," meaning it is no longer a new disease rapidly spreading, but one of a long list of viruses that all of us are exposed to.

---

[1] Sadaf Akhtar and Jane Barlow, "Forgiveness Therapy for the Promotion of Mental Well-Being: A Systematic Review and Meta-Analysis," *Trauma, Violence, & Abuse* 19, no. 1 (2018): 107–122, https://doi.10.117/1524838016637079.

We doctors have to stay current with the literature on COVID, the standards of care, and issues such as long COVID. If we pretend COVID no longer exists, we are not doing our jobs and we are not taking care of our patients.

Tessa Fitzgerald, RN, tried so hard to avoid COVID. She got her COVID vaccines. She wore her mask faithfully. She pushed through her fear of the disease to become the project manager at two of our testing projects. She led our testing team at the Washington State Fair in the fall of 2021. When the Puyallup tribe needed a testing site for their workers and others next to the large casino in Tacoma, Ellen from Pierce County asked for Tessa by name to be in charge. She persevered through the rain and the Omicron surge, when a seemingly endless line of cars wound off into the distance. Later, she wore a mask at the office long after we had made it optional. She was key to implementing so many projects for us—from monoclonal antibodies to the electronic medical record system needed for our telehealth program.

Tessa picked up a very mild case of COVID at a work party just after our last testing site closed in early 2023. A week or two later, she noticed a burning in her abdomen whenever she ate. This worsened to where she could pinpoint where the food was in her system by the fire that she felt inside, first near her lower right ribs, then progressing further down as the hours went by. She could barely eat and lost 40 pounds. She was afflicted with overwhelming fatigue and wound up in bed nearly 24 hours per day. She felt a thick brain fog where she could not concentrate, remember things, or sometimes even talk coherently. She couldn't process words on a page and became unable to read, one of her favorite pastimes. Randomly, while simply sitting, her Apple watch would alert her to a very rapid pulse of 160. Within a month, this high-energy person felt her body was only functioning at about 15%.

Tessa, married to a doctor and with good insurance, had an endless succession of examinations and medical tests, which found enteric neuropathy (disordered nerve signals in the gut) and POTS (postural orthostatic tachycardia syndrome). These diagnoses are more the result of something than an underlying cause. Without another unifying diagnosis, Tessa's problems were consistent with long COVID.[1] Still poorly understood, between one and ten percent of people infected with COVID developed this syndrome, which can last for years.[2]

Tessa, a young professional, was basically in bed, unable to work, run, or think clearly for about a year before she started to notice any improvement. Then, oh so gradually, the burning started to lessen. The rapid heart rate improved. After several months, she was able to do some volunteer work, as long as she could take a long nap every day. She started to gain weight. Her husband found a position in Arizona, where more access to the sun seemed to help. She is so happy to be able to run again and can now take full-day work shifts.

COVID vaccination helps prevent long COVID, but it still can happen, as Tessa's story shows. We in the medical field struggle to understand and treat it.

Our society carries around another post-COVID syndrome that is difficult to describe. Components include bitterness, anger, confusion, resentment, and an inability to maintain good connections with people who used to be close to us.

When I bring up the topic of COVID, and especially when I tell someone I am writing about it, I invariably get two responses. First, the person says, "Oh, people are over that, we have moved on. Why bother writing about it? Nobody is interested in that anymore." Then, after a pause, the person starts to describe his or her unique struggles during COVID, sometimes the story of how sick they were, the details of someone's death, or how crazy it was that people didn't wear masks or get the vaccine. Others review how they were traumatized by not being able to work or go to school, or how they are still mad at the government, the media, arrogant doctors, or mandatory quarantines or shots. Often, people add an emotional story about who they were frustrated with or which close friend or family member they no longer

---

[1] Trisha Greenhalgh et al., "Long COVID: a clinical update," *The Lancet* 404, no. 10453 (2024): 707–724, https://doi.org/10.1016/S0140-6736(24)01136-X.
[2] Xan Xie et al., "Postacute Sequelae of SARS-CoV-2 Infection in the Pre-Delta, Delta, and Omicron Eras," *New England Journal of Medicine* 391, no. 6 (2024):151–525, https://doi.org/10.1056/NEJMoa2403211.

talk to. I have learned to listen patiently because I have tapped into something they need to get off their chest. When I can maintain a nonjudgmental attitude (which can strain me to my limits), sometimes it seems a heavy weight drops off their spirit.

What can we do as individuals and as a society to treat this syndrome? When I think about my struggles to forgive, whether it is government and hospital leaders, anti-vax conspiracy theorists, pastors who did not encourage masks, or someone who just cut me off on the highway, I am reminded of an amazing woman I met years ago in Kenya.

I was waiting for my flight back to the States at the airport in Nairobi in 2006. I had just finished a few weeks of volunteer work at a small-town clinic about an hour north. I was fatigued and ready to get back to my family. But when I heard a woman talking French over by the souvenir shop, I thought this would be a good chance to practice my ever-amateur language abilities, so I wandered closer. There, I found a tall black woman who I guessed was in her late 40s. She was quite striking and could have been a model. After whoever she was talking to wandered off, we exchanged simple greetings in French. She rapidly changed to English because she was completely fluent, as well as kind, and we continued visiting.

"You know," she said after a while, "I am not sure why, but I really feel I should tell you this story that I do not typically share."

"OK," I replied, not sure where this was going.

"I am from Burundi, as I already mentioned," she started as I settled into listening mode. "My father was a diplomat. As I grew up, we were stationed in various countries, mostly in Europe. I learned many languages quickly—always had a knack for that.

"We were well off," she continued, "and enjoyed life and all the opportunities we had. I went to excellent schools. After college, I married a wonderful man and had a beautiful daughter. We settled into our life in the capital of Bujumbura. My husband worked in human rights, and we still traveled quite a bit. I was so proud of him and of my daughter, who was a fantastic companion and so easy to care for." She made sure she had my eyes and asked: "You know of the horrors in Rwanda, which were happening around that time?"

"Yes, I am familiar," I said, fearing what might be coming next.

More than 800,000 people were slaughtered in the Rwandan genocide of 1994.[1,2]

"Well, that craziness spread across the border, and friends told us it was not safe for my husband because of his advocacy work. Perhaps we should have left, but we thought the danger wasn't that great. The city seemed calm and safe.

"In any case, we were walking beside a park one Sunday afternoon. A van drove up next to us and stopped. I didn't think much of it until out jumped three guys with machine guns. Before I could blink, they riddled my husband and 10-year-old daughter with bullets, jumped back in the van, and sped away. In an instant, my family was taken from me forever."

She looked beyond me. Beyond the airport, I think. The story paused. She was not crying, but at the same time, she did not lack feeling. This strong woman wasn't pausing for effect.

A slight tilt of the head, and she was back with me. "I didn't tell you this for information. I wanted to give you a complete picture."

Did she just tell me only half the story? I thought. *Does it get worse?* I mumbled something in condolence, and she continued.

"I live in Quebec now. I have a good group of friends. I have a counselor. It has been difficult, but I am moving on."

"That's good," I offered meekly.

"But I knew something was missing. More than my family. The grief I have still, that is understandable. I will carry that burden for the rest of my life, though it has gotten a little lighter over the years. But there was something else, something I had to do."

"What was that?" I asked.

"Forgiveness," she said simply. She paused, and again she was somewhere else. I waited. I felt like I should take off my shoes for the holy ground or something. But that would have been weird in the

---

[1] "Rwanda genocide of 1994," *Encyclopedia Britannica*, February 10, 2025, https://www.britannica.com/event/Rwanda-genocide-of-1994.

[2] Roméo Dallaire, *Shake Hands with the Devil* (Grand Central Publishing, 2004). (Difficult emotionally to read, but a very good account, including of the social-political shift that undergirded the disaster.)

airport. Were others listening to this?

"I had to forgive them. I had to. Something was eating me from the inside. More than grief, other than grief, though tied to it. It was my bitterness and rage, my anger. It was more than a burden to carry, it was a hole in my side and my life blood was flowing out. Forgiveness was the only way."

"What did you do?" I asked.

"I went to my friends and my counselor. They all said the same thing: Do not forgive! You have to hold on to the anger, to fight for justice, to do the work of social advocacy. Harness that energy, don't lose it. Work through your grief, sure, but keep your anger and never forgive!"

I didn't know what to say. What could I say? Forget about that horror and let those people off the hook? Carry your bitterness down to the grave? An impossible question she faced, though apparently, she had come through it.

"I disagreed with them," she said sadly. "They are still my friends, but I disagreed. I wasn't going to find those men and let them hurt me, or free them from prison if that is where they are. But in my heart, I knew I had to forgive them. To see them as humans, sons, brothers. And I did. I forgave them. I was all alone, no family, friends disagreeing with me, but somehow, I knew it was what I had to do."

"Was it the right decision?" I asked.

As this woman in the airport looked at me, her face glowed and she smiled. "It was the most wonderful thing in my entire life," she said. "I still believe in justice. I still believe in advocacy work, in human rights. But I know what I know: forgiveness is the only way."

You might think that since that evening in the airport, after hearing the words of Jesus translated by an African linguist to my Western ears, I would surely follow. Yet every day I struggle. From my anger at the millions of deaths from COVID, to minor annoyances with my wife, I let that same hole develop that my friend was talking about, and I forget the blessing of forgiving others.

When I am secure in God as my father, and know my own sins and flaws are forgiven by the sacrifice of Jesus on the cross, I can pause racing around to shore up my identity and take a place of humility. Then I can see much more clearly the next challenge that lies before me:

forgiveness of others. This is an unequivocal assignment that Jesus gave all his followers: forgive everyone who does any sort of wrong against you,[1] a message repeated almost to the point of absurdity by his disciples and St. Paul.[2]

What other steps are there, related to forgiveness, that we as a society can take, as we try to heal from COVID?

---

[1] Mark 11:25, Luke 6:37, Matthew 6:14–15, Luke 17:3–4
[2] Only a few of the references: Colossians 3:13, I John 1:9, I Peter 4:8, Acts 7:59–60

Chapter Twenty-Eight: Healing Us

He has shown you, O mortal, what is good. And what does the Lord require of you? To act justly and to love mercy and to walk humbly with your God.

– Micah 6:8 (NIV)

The quality of mercy is not strained
It droppeth as the gentle rain from heaven
Upon the place beneath. It is twice blest–
It blesseth him that gives, and him that takes.

– William Shakespeare[1]

When I look at my country right now, I see division, anger, extremism, and a clamoring after numbing distractions. I do not see a society united in seeking truth, the common good, or wellbeing. I do not see us trying to help those who are less well-off. It is like we are suffering with a sort of post-COVID sickness on a national scale.

Studies have shown that counseling and exercise help long COVID symptoms,[2] the problem that Tessa suffered with in the last chapter. Sometimes simple actions help, even though the original problem is

---

[1] William Shakespeare, *Merchant of Venice* (Washington Square Press: 1990), 72.
[2] Dena Zeraatkar et al., "Interventions for the management of long covid (post-covid condition): living systematic review," *British Medical Journal* 387 (2024), https://doi.org/10.1136/bmj-2024-081318.

complex and difficult to trace or define. As I consider what we all lived through during those three years of COVID, I believe there are three things we all can do to help find healing for ourselves and for our society: process our grief, humbly listen to others, and forgive those who have hurt us.

If you have lost someone to COVID or otherwise, it makes sense to work on grief recovery, and possibly you are in a grief support group or you have gone to a counsellor. But often grief persists as a powerful force and life disruptor, even though enough time has passed that you think you should have healed. Even if you didn't lose someone to COVID, you may still be grieving. The COVID years took other things besides lives from us—freedoms, friendships, graduations, life plans, stability, and more. We can be grieving those losses without realizing it, puzzled over our depression and anger, not knowing where to focus it. *The Grief Recovery Handbook* explains:

> Grief is the normal and natural reaction to loss of any kind. Therefore, the feelings you are having are also normal and natural for you. The problem is that we have all been socialized to believe that these feelings are abnormal and unnatural. While grief is normal and natural, and clearly the most powerful of all emotions, it is also the most neglected and misunderstood experience, often by both the grievers and those around them.[1]

Many of the people that I worked with during that time were already wrestling with grief that had nothing to do with COVID—related to job loss, divorce, bad choices and their results, loss of a child, and other issues. Some of these folks had enormous grief that had paralyzed them previously, but they had processed their loss and sadness enough to get to a point where they wanted to help others, and they wound up working for me or with me. I was honored to see their progress and how they were able to thrive and give despite what they

---

[1] I strongly recommend this book to those going through grief: John James and Russell Friedman, *The Grief Recovery Handbook: The Action Program for Moving Beyond Death, Divorce, and Other Losses, including Health, Career, and Faith*, 20th Anniversary Expanded Edition (HarperCollins, 2009), 3.

had gone through. They showed me what it looks like to do grief work instead of sweeping it under the rug.

In chapter 10, I told the story of Dr. Mary Ellen Biggerstaff's ability to humbly listen to others as we planned and how that helped lead to the successful mass vaccination project in Lewis County. Dr. Biggerstaff did not have that unhealthy humility that says, I am a nobody, please step on me. She is strong and vocal in her beliefs and opinions.[1] No, she had that humility that is core to a moral character, the result of learning and hard work, that sees value in learning from others. A humility that says, I listen to you because I respect you, your identity, your thoughts, and your feelings. You have worth!

Listening well is indispensable to finding the common ground necessary for working together toward healing. For example, we can find common ground in affirming the importance of public health, even if we disagree on what should be mandated versus what should be advised. Our work in Lewis County and elsewhere demonstrated how people who disagree can work well together, and how persistence, hard work, and determination make a difference in people's lives.

We as a society have to move towards Dr. Biggerstaff's approach and away from that of many radio hosts and podcasters who listen just enough to introduce a topic and then angrily rant about how bad the world is and how my group or my theory or my story is more important than the rest of you losers. If further discussion is allowed, it is only to stir up a yelling match. Rather than encouraging listening, this format promotes a way of thinking that makes us all deaf to each other and hamstrings us in building true community.

Jesus said, "All those who exalt themselves will be humbled, and those who humble themselves will be exalted."[2] It takes spiritual strength to be a good listener, as the benefits are not always immediate.

Forgiveness is the third treatment I would prescribe for the healing

---

[1] Dr. Biggerstaff has since written a book about people who stand up for their beliefs: Mary Ellen Biggerstaff, *Radical Nurses: 28 Stories of Resistance, Reform, & Revolution* (Bildung Press: 2024).
[2] Luke 14:11 (NIV)

of our society. It may be the hardest treatment to undergo and could be viewed as the last of a series of steps. First, we must walk through our own grief and anger, then humbly listen to others and see their pains and hurts. As my friend from Burundi showed, forgiveness may require several years of emotional work. And it is important to point out what forgiveness is not.

Forgiveness is not trust. For broken trust to be restored, it must be earned with changed behavior over time. Too many times, I have seen people go back to abusive situations because they feel like or they have been told that they must "forgive" someone, which they think means ignoring ongoing abuse. They then don't take steps necessary to protect themselves and their children.

Forgiveness is not forgetting. Responsible people do not pretend something did not happen and has no consequences. This area can be tricky and often requires wise counsel from others to sort through. It takes great spiritual strength and discernment to hate the sin and love the sinner.[1]

Forgiveness is not reconciliation. It is a prerequisite for reconciliation, but reconciliation is possible only when both parties are committed to it. Forgiveness is not flipping a switch and deciding not to be angry anymore. We don't have direct control over our emotions, so we can't just choose to stop having a feeling. To forgive, I identify what the offender owes me or what I feel he owes me—an apology (private and/or public), restitution, empathy, remorse, or actions that reveal a change of heart. Then, having named what is owed, I cancel the debt. I say in my heart: This person no longer owes this to me. And I no longer expect it from them.[2] Emotions are part of this, of course, but must follow, not lead, the journey. As for COVID and forgiveness, we don't need to, nor should we, take the blame for other people's bad choices. But that bitterness we are holding on to?

---

[1] Mohandas *Gandhi, Gandhi, An Autobiography: The Story of My Experiments with Truth* (Beacon Press, 1993), 276.
[2] I appreciate Pastor Eddy Hall for help with this assessment of what forgiveness is not.

Refusing to forgive is bad for our mental health[1] and does nothing to resolve the problem.

Are you angry at God? There is so much evil in the world that many of us are left scratching our heads: how could a good God let these things happen? Is it wrong to be mad at God? The Bible does not whitewash this issue—David, Jonah, Job, and Jeremiah were all angry with God. Pastor Walter Wangerin addresses these difficult questions in my other favorite book about grief, *Mourning into Dancing*. He encourages us to tell God just how angry we are and why. "God is our final antagonist,"[2] he says, since God is the creator of all things. He says to direct our anger towards God openly and tell him about it, because (1) we often harmfully direct our anger towards others when ultimately we are angry at God, (2) though we often deny it, we think God is responsible for the problem, and (3) God can take it: "God, who understands us better than we understand ourselves, will not be destroyed by our most passionate rages… [God] is glad for the chance to communicate."[3]

In church, Christians take the elements of Holy Communion and remember the death of Jesus on the cross. This reflects an eternal truth: that we deserve punishment and eternal death, but God sent his son to die on the cross as a substitute. This is God forgiving us so we can forgive others.

Beyond its tragic toll of physical illness and death, the COVID pandemic inflicted enormous emotional and relational wounds. I leave you with a prescription for the healing of our broken society: grieve well, listen humbly to each other, and forgive.

May we choose this path of healing as we remember and honor those three years.

---

[1] Loren Toussaint et al., "Late Adulthood, COVID-19-Related Stress Perceptions, Meaning in Life, and Forgiveness as Predictors of Mental Health During the COVID-19 Pandemic," *Frontiers in Psychology* 12 (2021), https://doi.org/10.3389/fpsyg.2021.731017.
[2] Walter Wangerin, *Mourning Into Dancing* (Zondervan, 1992), 222.
[3] Ibid.

Acknowledgements

Thank you to God who walked me through those years and was with me. Thank you to my wife, Jennifer, who, against her better judgment, decided to support me in writing this story down, and then bore with me when the process took month after month longer than anticipated. I appreciate Eddy Hall, who, with endless patience, brought me back from the edge in my writing and made the whole thing much more readable. Dr. Rick Sams, you are the greatest friend anyone could want. Thanks for all the advice! There is no way Bird's Eye Medical could have been possible without Patrick Hastings, ever-capable businessman and scholar of everything. David, Erika, and Nathan, I didn't deserve such amazing progeny; you rescued us multiple times during the pandemic. Thank you to everyone who worked for, volunteered through, or otherwise partnered with Bird's Eye Medical. Each one of you is unique, incredible, and fascinating. You gave of yourselves to help others during that historic time. Thank you for letting me see a piece of your sacrifice that I know God sees and will honor.

Gloria Kaczmarksi saw the need and became a great nursing leader for the Lewis County mass vaccinations. Carolyn Standen was such a stalwart wherever she went, and she went everywhere. Erika Taylor, human resources expert, is such a practical, resourceful, and supportive person. Edith Kimani served well and with vigor in several areas of administration. Dr. Angela Tobias never missed a beat when she gave shots, counsel, and energy to the project. Dr. Rachel Wood was the hardworking public health doctor in Lewis County, who was always supportive. Patty Baxer, nurse practitioner and world traveler, always had insights and energy. Jacob Johnson was a towering powerhouse on several projects, literally and figuratively. Dr. Heidi Greene gave selflessly of her time and energy. Jessica Labrum carried a heavy load throughout, from testing and computers to the records wrap-up. David Lockard saved us from many a computer disaster and was a great IT resource for the company. Jorum Mwangi did every task with diligence, including endless driving of supplies over mile after mile. Dr. Christina Schofield was such a great support as I called her for infectious disease help. Adam Oskvig, young accountant and pilot, was essential to keeping track of the money and was such a blessing to my wife in his attentive and patient work. Alfredo Urueta was an energy-filled firecracker and logged more hours and miles than possibly anyone else. Lawrence Kinnaman was such a positive and upbeat person and manager. Sharron Ferraro, nurse practitioner, was able to do a fantastic job as telehealth clinician and helped lead the provider team while also juggling a newborn and her husband's military work. Ashley Burnham was key to the success of the Greyhound station testing site. Besides sewing caps, Laying Hou worked in various locations and encouraged many.

Thank you to all the owners of and workers at the places where I ensconced myself to write, with a special thanks to Anytime Toffee and Coffee shop, the public library, and Woods Coffee, all in Ferndale, Washington, where we have now moved. Also, the Pa Klang Mueang Café in Khon Kaen, Thailand, with its supportive and overwhelmingly creative owner.

Thank you to those who gave us Christian fellowship when it was difficult, and we had to be creative. Thanks to the Christian Medical Association and our small local Zoom group. Thanks to Youhan Hou for starting a Pathways[1] Bible study. Thank you to the pastors and members at Westwood Baptist, Olympia Chinese Christian Church, and Hillcrest Church in Bellingham. Thanks to Pastor Christian Lindbeck, who gave wise counsel at the right time.

I have to thank all the doctors, nurses, and administrators at Providence Hospice. I especially appreciate Dr. Tagest Hailu, Dr. Lauri Powers, and Dr. Tracy Stearns-Church for getting me started and being

---

[1] Based on the book: *Alan Lewis, Pathways Bible Study Method: A Better Way to do Bible Study* (CreateSpace: 2015).

such great colleagues. Carlos Aliniz was an amazing leader during that difficult time in the hospice world.

Thank you to all the people who have helped me to improve my writing over the years, including Dr. Robert Abrams, who is now Professor Emeritus at the University of Washington, and Sue Loeffler, who edited and gave me so much feedback over several years before this project. Thanks to my professors at Faith University who pushed me, especially Dr. Jay Diller and Dr. James Tille. Thank you to Ken Jones, who coached and inspired me. Thank you to Megan Waldner, an amazing proofreader. I appreciate my sister Jennifer Thye (she uses "Jennifer Bunge" for her artist name), who helped with formatting and the cover art, and is a fantastic artist overall. Thanks to other creatively inspiring people like doctor-poet John Shaw and pediatrician George Tsao. Thank you to the Northwest Christian Writers Association and its leadership for help and guidance. Thanks to my mother, Rebecca Bunge Eisert, for instilling a love of books. Thanks to my father, David Bunge, who showed me how a humble life of service, even when cut short, has infinite value, and who always pointed me to God.

Permissions

English Bible Translations:

www.ingramcontent.com/pod-product-compliance
Lightning Source LLC
Chambersburg PA
CBHW030521100426
42813CB00001B/108